The Spokesman
Brown Studies
Edited by Ken Coates

Published by Spokesman for the
Bertrand Russell Peace Foundation

Spokesman 97   2008

CONTENTS

Editorial: Browned Off	3	Ken Coates
Breaking Storm?	8	Gabriel Kolko
Planned Economy	11	Gordon Brown
Brown's Direction?	17	Paul Rogers
Prospects for Labour	23	Jim Mortimer
New Beginnings?	27	Joe Marino
My Friend Vonnegut	31	Ralph Steadman
My Last Word	33	Kurt Vonnegut Interviewed by J. Rentilly
Socialist Aim	38	Jean Jaurès
Jaurès	40	Leon Trotsky
Erasing the Past	45	John Berger
America at Point Zero	49	Gabriel Kolko
Blackwater	53	Kevin Cahill
Star Wars	57	David Webb Theodore Postol
Scotland against Nukes	65	Alex Salmond MSP
	67	Rob Edwards
Dossier	69	Russell Tribunal on Palestine UN Should Leave Quartet Bush & Aznar Talk War Osama bin Laden
Reviews	79	Michael Barratt Brown, Ken Coates, Glen Rangwala, Stan Newens. Peter Jackson, John Daniels

Cover with thanks to Steve Bell
Printed by the Russell Press Ltd., Nottingham, UK

ISSN 0262 7922   ISBN 978 0 85124 750 2

Subscriptions
Institutions £35.00
Individuals £20.00 (UK)
£25.00 (ex UK)

Back issues available on request

A CIP catalogue record for this book is available from the British Library

Published by the
Bertrand Russell Peace Foundation Ltd.,
Russell House
Bulwell Lane
Nottingham NG6 0BT
England
Tel. 0115 9784504
email:
elfeuro@compuserve.com
www.spokesmanbooks.com
www.russfound.org

Editorial Board:
Michael Barratt Brown
Ken Coates
John Daniels
Ken Fleet
Stuart Holland
Tony Simpson

Routledge Classics

Get inside one of the greatest minds of the Twentieth Century

BERTRAND RUSSELL TITLES

History of Western Philosophy
Bertrand Russell

'Should never be out of print.'
— The Evening Standard

1136pp: 978-0-415-32505-9: **£12.99**

Sceptical Essays
Bertrand Russell

With a new preface by John Gray

'Bertrand Russell wrote the best English prose of any twentieth-century philosopher.' — The Times

240pp: 978-0-415-32508-0: **£9.99**

In Praise of Idleness
Bertrand Russell

With a new introduction by **Anthony Gottlieb**

'There is not a page that does not provoke argument and thought.'
— The Sunday Times

192pp: 978-0-415-32506-6: **£8.99**

Why I Am Not a Christian
Bertrand Russell

With a new introduction by **Simon Blackburn**

'Devastating in its use of cold logic.'
— The Independent

272pp: 978-0-415-32510-3: **£9.99**

Power
Bertrand Russell

With a new introduction by **Samuel Brittan**

'Extremely penetrating analysis of human nature in politics.'
— The Sunday Times

288pp: 978-0-415-32507-3: **£9.99**

(New)

The Conquest of Happiness
Bertrand Russell

With a new preface by A.C. Grayling

'He writes what he calls common sense, but is in fact uncommon wisdom.'
— The Observer

200pp: 978-0-415-37847-5: **£9.99**

an **informa** business

www.routledge.com/classics   Available from all good bookshops

Editorial
Browned Off

Although it had been gradually dawning over recent years, there has now been a sudden flash of general realisation that Mrs. Thatcher has gone on and on and on. Now it is crystal clear. Many people thought a long time ago that Tony Blair was a continuator of all the essential principles of Thatcherism, only more ruthless and, if possible, less sentimental. But this realisation has become inescapable, because it is now clear as crystal that Gordon Brown is cast in exactly the same mould.

Over recent years, his jockeying for position has from time to time meant that he has developed an appearance of difference from Blatcherism. True, he has made different speeches at Labour Conferences, and remained sensitive to various elements in old Labour rhetoric. But watching him appearing at the Trade Union Congress in 2007, and following his resolute despatch of low-paid public sector workers with a below inflation imposed settlement in their pay, we cannot fail to be aware of his benign approach to the bonuses of major company directors. Equality of outcome is nowhere to be seen.

Half the population in Britain today, taken together, earns only one-third of the combined income of three per cent of our fattest cats.

Manifestly the age of Thatcher will one day come to an end, and that may be soon. It cannot be sustained, and it is only tolerated because the entire political class has been corrupted in its presence. The result of this corruption manifests itself in various disintegrations. In England, the disintegration most visibly affects the social fabric, as parts of the underclass arm themselves for ferocious shootouts with rival contenders, and children knife one another at school. Gang warfare breaks out in our cities, as drug lords assert their sway over entire territories. Social disintegration makes increasing areas of our cities uninhabitable for the respectable poor, whose wages are frozen while their problems intensify.

Things are apparently different in Scotland, where an authentic Social Democrat has come to head the Government, as the Scottish Nationalists have provided an area of genuine, if restricted, choice for a people much put upon by the indignities of Blatcherism. The justified hatred of Thatcher in Scottish coalfields will yet cause trouble for her most recent host in Downing Street, whose constituency suffered grievously from her depredations.

Before the downfall of Tony Blair, Richard Brooks, the Fabian Research Director, asked if it were time for a further revision of the Labour Party's Constitution, rectifying the new Clause IV. This consists of such anodyne verbiage that it is unlikely that any politician would want to alter it, running the risk of accidentally making an actual commitment to do something or go somewhere.

The revised Clause IV is such babble that it will be impossible to refine it without running the risk of meaning something. The reason for Blair's constitutional reform was claimed to be that the original Clause, as drafted by Sydney Webb, promised one or another form of public ownership of the means of production, distribution and exchange. It has been universally forgotten that this undertaking, which was by some people thought a little rash, had already been extensively revised by the incorporation of an addendum drafted under the influence of Hugh Gaitskell, which merely insisted on the maintenance of a mixed economy. It does not cross Mr. Brooks' mind to ask where the mixed economy went. But since the annulment of the Labour Party's commitment to socialism, it has become clear why the mixed economy perished at the same time as public ownership of production, distribution and exchange. The new firm was just as committed against the revisionist aim as it was against the original Ark of the Covenant. Neither Tony Blair nor Gordon Brown wanted any truck with a mixed economy, because it was their avowed intention to privatise all of it. The New Labour project was about eliminating public ownership in any form, and establishing the complete, final and total domination of the market place.

That is why Richard Brooks finds 'equality is a difficult issue, both in theory and practice'. In a market society, inequality is an absolute precondition of economic activity. Competition rules, and where competition is the main motor of activity, some win, and this needs others to lose. As the losers become more and more numerous, the winners become more and more rich. As democracy wanes, the military needs to wax.

> 'Why' asks Richard Brooks, 'should a child born into poverty have worse health, poorer education prospects, a higher risk of being a victim of crime and a shorter life expectancy than one born to middle class parents? It might be argued that the right objective is not equality but minimum standards for all – and never mind what happens to those who are more fortunate.'

Alas, this is not obvious to the majority of Party members, continues the Fabian researcher. We need to come to a better understanding of this issue, or risk the return 'to a situation where the members no longer believe in the stated objectives of the Party'.

It might be thought that if the members no longer believed in babble, that this could represent a useful step forward. But this is not the present day Fabian belief. Modern political Parties are prototype advertising agencies, selling access to the sources of power. The only problem with babble as a stock in trade, they believe, is that people might cease to believe it, so that the creative task that must be faced is the constant renewal of its credibility.

Perhaps this might not need so much renewal if it stayed closer to political realities, but this could mean diluting the babble quotient and opening a dangerous window on truth. Original Fabians knew that the approach to equality was difficult, and Bernard Shaw once even claimed that he favoured precise mathematical equality and could see no justification for anything else. More pragmatic Fabians believed in the inevitability of gradualness, and preached an approach to equality which could, perhaps slowly, render us all more equal than we used to be.

The Russian Revolution learned from this principle and insisted that Communist Party members apply a rule in which the wealthiest drew no more than four times the remuneration of the poorest. This differential could be (and

> Nothing, therefore, is really in question, or ever has been, but the differences between class incomes. Already there is economic equality between captains, and economy equality between cabin boys. What is at issue still is whether there shall be economic equality between captains and cabin boys. What would Jesus have said? Presumably he would have said that if your only object is to produce a captain and a cabin boy for the purpose of transferring you from Liverpool to New York, or to manoeuvre a fleet and carry powder from the magazine to the gun, then you need give no more than a shilling to the cabin boy for every pound you give to the more expensively trained captain. But if in addition to this you desire to allow the two human souls which are inseparable from the captain and the cabin boy and which alone differentiate them from the donkey-engine, to develop all their possibilities, then you may find the cabin boy's work does not do so much for the soul as the captain's work. Consequently you will have to give him at least as much as the captain unless you definitely wish him to be a lower creature, in which case the sooner you are hanged as an abortionist the better.
>
> George Bernard Shaw
> Preface to *Androcles and the Lion*

was) varied by allowing greater differentials: but it could also, in principle, be varied by narrowing the gap. But there is no way in the world that old Fabians could have bought into current Labour doctrine on the income distribution appropriate to modern economies.

Of course, a crucial argument for public ownership was that it was believed to facilitate the narrowing of differentials, on the grounds that democratic ownership would tend to restrict the rewards of leaders to levels more acceptable to the led. The good manager might be worth a premium to the collective: but that premium would not exceed the rational expectations of those over whom his or her managerial talents were to be exercised. To give the boss twice your wages would seem to many cooperative workers to be more than generous, and the Russian rule that they be given wider differential of up to four times would seem excessive. But Gordon Brown's rule that the wheels of industry will stop if the fat cats are not given a hundred times the rewards of normal people, could not be defended anywhere.

At the beginning of October 2007, *The Independent* reported:

> 'The bonanza in boardroom pay has become even more spectacular, according to the latest figures from the accountancy firm KPMG. The typical chief executive of a FTSE 100 company has seen their total remuneration rise by 12 per cent in the past year, to reach over £2.6m. That's four times the rate of increase in average earnings, leaving the business élite on pay over 100 times what most of their employees earn.'[1]

That is why the babble industry has done so very well, because few have the ability to provide a coherent justification for inequality on the modern scale, and without sufficient babble to anaesthetize the sound of injustice you will one day need a very large army. Alas, at present, that is all away, playing the Great Game in the wastes of Helmand, or learning the arts of self-defence in Basra's airport.

Behind the babble, somebody does the actual counting. Alan Greenspan recently told the *Financial Times* (17 September 2007) that there was one very odd feature in the 'global market nirvana' which characterises today's economy, to wit:

> 'Profits are much higher than they should be in a world of ever intensifying global competition.'

Greenspan says:

> 'We know in an accounting sense what is causing it. The share of worker compensation in national income in the US and some other developed countries is unusually low by historical standards. But we don't know in an economic sense what the processes are.' In the long run, he says, 'real compensation tends to parallel real productivity, and we have seen that for generations, but not now. It has veered off course for reasons I am not clear about.'

The *Financial Times* reports that Mr. Greenspan expects some normalisation of profit and wage shares, but he remains puzzled about why the proportions have shifted.

> 'He worries that if wages for the average US worker do not start to rise more quickly political support for free markets may be undermined.'

So it may, indeed, be time to revisit Clause IV.

A loud knock on the door was heard during the Northern Rock crisis, when the much-celebrated independence of the Bank of England seemed to have been overruled by Government intervention in order to guarantee personal savings in that beleaguered bank. Commentators were quick to point out that this amounted to a decision to nationalise the Bank. Up to a point, Lord Copper. But it does without doubt amount to a dilution of the pure essence of Thatcherite doctrine. And if the crisis which has already visited the United States, Germany, Spain and Ireland does not go away, but actually intensifies, what other interventions may prove necessary?

No doubt these matters might have impinged on the discussions between the Prime Minister and Mr. Greenspan during his visit to Downing Street[2]. Attempts to explain the remarkable story of the General Election that never was have tended to hinge on allegations of electoral opportunism. Mr. Brown, it had been said, was enjoying a surge of support, a 'bounce' which put him strongly in the lead in the polls. All this had been a very abrupt development, but it was to be quickly matched by an equally abrupt transformation, in which Mr. Cameron was to appear the runaway success story, while the Prime Minister's poll scorings fell further and further away. On the surface, this seems to offer a reasonable if unflattering explanation for what happened. But the futurology of polls is a less than reliable indicator of likely outcomes. And what *was* Mr. Greenspan telling his friend during that visit?

The *Financial Times* (26 September 2007) was quite lonely in insisting that:

> 'As Gordon Brown attempts to read the election runes, statistics charting the outlook for the UK economy will consume the Prime Minister almost as much as polling data from key marginal seats.'

There are already many economic numbers freely available, to sustain arguments for and against an early election. But the *Financial Times* is right when it says that:

> 'The big "what if?" that may keep the Prime Minister awake at night, however, is whether Northern Rock was an exception or a sign of a generalised malaise in the management of the British economy.'

Gabriel Kolko already posted a warning in his article for *The Spokesman* (see below, pages 8-10). But is it likely that Alan Greenspan was not alive to all these issues? And is it not possible that what tilted Gordon Brown towards an early election was precisely the anticipation of severely turbulent economic weather to come?

The resurgence of Conservative support made any such calculation problematic. If Labour could prepare for bad times to come with a runaway election victory, even one secured only in the nick of time, opportunity would certainly knock. But if Labour were to reap a setback, even a hung Parliament, this would not help in the least in the negotiation of hard economic times to come.

We are not privy to the thoughts of Mr. Greenspan, and we don't know about the apparently feverish changes of mind in Downing Street during those troubled days. But it does seem, on balance, that economic uncertainty, and political turbulence, are on their way back among us.

How long will it be before the ethos of public intervention, or indeed of public enterprise, also begins to reappear among us?

Ken Coates

Notes

1 Sean O'Grady elaborates further:
'In the case of those chief executives still in post, their income went up by 16 per cent, accelerating last year's 9 per cent rise. The chief executive of one of the smaller FTSE 250 companies would expect to see a total package of just over £1m, up from £878,000 in 2006. Britain's top corporate earner is probably still Bob Diamond of Barclays Capital, who took home £22.9m last year, including a performance-related bonus of £10.4m. Others in that bracket include Bart Becht, chief executive of Reckitt Benckiser, the man behind Mr Sheen, on £22m; Giles Thorley, head of Punch Taverns, making ends meet on £11m; and Lord Browne, late of BP, similarly well-looked after. Mr Thorley's package is equivalent to 1,147 of his staff's pay. Taken together, the directors of FTSE 100 companies collectively earned £515m last year – exceeding the GDP of the likes of Eritrea and the Seychelles. Looking around the boardroom, we find the average FTSE 100 finance director can expect to see around £1.4m land in his bank account, with other executive directors on around £1.2m. For the FTSE 250, the equivalent figures are £623,000 and £544,000.'

2 This visit, which took place on Monday 17 September 2007, was part of a concerted series of meetings with the American financial establishment. Visits were received from the Chairman of the US Federal Reserve, Ben Bernanke, on Friday 21 September, and Henry Paulson, the US Treasury Secretary, who met with Chancellor Darling and the French Finance Minister, also on 17 September. It seems that the British were being persuaded to intervene more directly in the crisis of Northern Rock.

Has the Storm Broken?

Gabriel Kolko

Gabriel Kolko warned of the 'Crisis of Greed' in Spokesman 92. *Here he develops his analysis of the convulsions of global finance.*

Contradictions now wrack the world's financial system, and a growing consensus exists between those who endorse it and those who argue the status quo is both crisis-prone as well as immoral. If we are to believe the institutions and personalities who have been in the forefront of the defence of capitalism, we are on the verge of a serious crisis – if not now, then in the near future.

The International Monetary Fund (IMF), the Bank for International Settlements, the British Financial Services Authority, the *Financial Times*, and innumerable mainstream commentators were increasingly worried, and publicly warned against many of the financial innovations that have now imploded. Warren Buffett, whom Forbes ranks the second richest man in the world, last year called credit derivatives – only one of the many new banking inventions – 'financial weapons of mass destruction'. Very conservative institutions and people predicted the upheaval in global finances we are today experiencing.

The IMF has taken the lead in criticizing the new international financial structure, and over the past three years it has published numerous detailed reasons why it has become so dangerous to the world's economic stability. Events have confirmed its prognostication that complexity and lack of transparency, the obscurity of risks and universal uncertainty, especially regarding collateralized debt and loan obligations, will cause a flight to security that will dry up much of the liquidity of banking.

'… Financial innovation itself', as a *Financial Times* columnist put it, 'is the problem'. The ultra-creative system is seizing up because no one understands where risks are located or how it works. It began to do so this summer and fixing it is not very likely.

It is impossible to measure the extent of the losses. The final results of this deluge have yet to be calculated. Even many of the players who have stakes in the countless arcane investment instruments are utterly ignorant. The sums are enormous.

Only a few of the many measures give us a rough estimate. The present crisis began – it has scarcely ended there – with sub-prime mortgage loans in the United Stares, which were valued at over $1.3 trillion at the beginning of 2007, but are, for practical purposes, worth far, far less today. We can ignore the impact of this crisis on US housing prices, but some projections are of a 10 per cent decline – another trillion or so. Indirectly, of course, the mortgage crisis has also brought many millions of people into the larger financial world and they will get badly hurt.

What the sub-prime market did was unleash a far greater maelstrom involving banks in Germany, France, Asia, and throughout the world, calling into question much of the world financial system as it has developed over the past decade.

Investment banks hold about $300 billion in private equity debts they planned to place – mainly in leveraged buy-outs. They will be forced to sell them at discounts or keep them on their balance sheets – either way they will lose.

The near-failure of the German Sachsen LB bank, which had to be saved from bankruptcy with 17.3 billion euros in credit, revealed that European banks hold over half a trillion dollars in so-called asset backed commercial paper, much of it in the United States and sub-prime mortgages. A failure in America caused Europe, too, to face a crisis. The problem is scarcely isolated.

The leading victims of this upheaval are the hedge funds. What are hedge funds? There are about 10,000 and, all told, they do everything. Some hedge funds, however, provided companies with capital and successfully competed with commercial banks because they took much greater risks. A substantial proportion are simple gamblers; some even bet on the weather – hunches. Many look to their computers and mathematics for models to guide their investments, and these have lost the most money, but funds based on other strategies also lost during August. The spectacular Long-term Capital Management 1998 failure was also due to its reliance on ingenious mathematical propositions, yet no one learned any lessons from it, proving that appeals to reason, as well as experience, fall on deaf ears if there is money to be made.

Some gained during the August crisis but more lost, and in the aggregate the hedge funds lost a great deal – their allure of rapid riches gone. There have been some spectacular bankruptcies and bailouts, including some of the biggest investment firms. Investors who got cold feet found that withdrawing money from hedge funds was nigh on impossible. The real worth of their holdings is hotly contested, and valuations vary wildly. In reality, there is no way to appraise them realistically – they all depend largely on what people want to believe and will take, or the market.

We are at the end of an era, living through the worst financial panic in many decades. Now begins global financial instability. It is impossible to speculate how long today's turmoil will last – but there now exists an uncertainty and lack of confidence that has been unparalleled since the 1930s – and this ignorance and fear is itself a crucial factor. The moment of reckoning for bankers and bosses has arrived. What is very clear is that losses are massive and the entire developed world is now experiencing the worst economic crisis since 1945, one in which troubles in one nation compound those in others.

All central banks are wracked by dilemmas. They have neither the resources nor the knowledge, including legal powers, to remedy the present maelstrom. Although there is clamour from financiers and assorted operators to bail them out, the Federal Reserve must also weigh the consequences of its moves, above all for inflation. Then there is the question of 'moral hazard'. Is it the Federal Reserve's responsibility to save financial adventurers from their own follies? Throughout August, the American and European central banks plunged about half a trillion dollars into the banking system in an attempt to unfreeze blocked credit and loans that followed the sub-prime crisis – an event which triggered a 'flight to safety' which greatly reduced banks' willingness to loan. In effect, the Federal Reserve relied on banks to restore confidence in the financial system, subsidizing their efforts.

Central banks' efforts succeeded only very partially but, in the aggregate, they failed: banks and investors now seek security rather than risk, and they will sit on their money. The Federal Reserve privately acknowledges its inability to cope with an inordinately complex financial structure. European central bankers are in exactly the same dilemma: they simply don't know what to do.

But this scarcely touches the real problem, which is structural and impinges wholly on the way the world financial structure has evolved over the past two decades. As in the past, there is a critical split in the banking and finance world and each has political leverage along with clashing interests. More important, central banks were not designed to cope with today's realities and have neither the legal powers nor knowledge to control them.

In this context, central banks will have increasing problems and the solutions they propose, as in the past, will be utterly inadequate, not because their intentions are wrong but because it is impossible to regulate such a vast, complex economy – even less today than in the past because there is no international mechanism to do so. Internationalization of finance has meant less regulation than ever, and regulation was scarcely very effective even at the national level.

Not only leftists are naïve but so, too, are those conservatives who think they can speak truth to power and change the course of events. Greed's only bounds are what makes money. Neither existing international institutions – of which the International Monetary Fund is the most important – nor well-intentioned advice will change this reality.

Wanted: A Planned Economy

Gordon Brown

These excerpts are taken from Gordon Brown's introduction to The Red Paper on Scotland, *which he edited for publication in 1975. The full text of this introduction is available from Spokesman as a Socialist Renewal pamphlet under the title* Lost, Stolen or Strayed?: Gordon Brown as Socialist Pretender *(£3 including postage).*

... Two themes are integral and complementary in the [*Red Paper*]. The first is that the social and economic problems confronting Scotland arise not from national suppression nor from London mismanagement (although we have had our share of both) but from the uneven and uncontrolled development of capitalism, and the failure of successive governments to challenge and transform it. Thus we cannot hope to resolve such problems merely by recovering a lost independence or through inserting another tier of government: what is required is planned control of our economy and a transformation of democracy at all levels. The second theme is more basic than that. We suggest the real resources of Scotland are not the reserves of oil beneath the sea (nor the ingenuity of native entrepreneurs) but the collective energies and potential of our people whose abilities and capacities have been stultified by a social system which has for centuries sacrificed social aspirations to private ambitions. It is argued that what appear to be contradictory features of Scottish life today – militancy and apathy, cynicism and a thirst for change – can best be understood as working people's frustration with and refusal to accept powerlessness and lack of control over blind social forces which determine their lives. It is a disenchantment which underlines an untapped potential for cooperative action upon which we must build.

The vision of the early socialists was of a society which had abolished for ever the dichotomy – the split personality caused by people's unequal control over their social development – between man's personal and collective existence, by substituting communal co-operation for the divisive forces of competition. Today the logic of present economic development, in inflation and stagnation, and at the same time the demand for the fullest use of material resources, makes it increasingly impossible to manage the economy both for private profit and the needs of society as a whole. Yet the long-standing paradox of Scottish politics has been the surging forward of working class industrial and political pressure (and in particular the loyal support given to Labour) and its containment through the accumulative failures of successive Labour Governments. More than fifty years ago socialism was a qualitative concept, an urgently felt moral imperative, about social control (and not merely state control or more or less equality). Today for many it means little more than a scheme for compensating the least fortunate in an unequal society. We suggest that the rise of modern Scottish nationalism is less an assertion of Scotland's permanence as a nation than a response to Scotland's uneven development – in particular to the gap between people's experiences as part of an increasingly demoralised Great Britain and their (oil-fired) expectations at a Scottish level. Thus, the discontent is a measure of both Scottish and British socialists to advance far and fast enough in shifting the balance of wealth and power to working people and in raising people's awareness – especially outside the central belt of Scotland in areas where inequalities are greater – about the co-operative possibilities for modern society ...

Social Needs

Any study of Scotland today must start from where people are, the realities of day-to-day living, extremes of wealth and poverty, unequal opportunities at work, in housing, health, education and community living generally. The gross inequalities which disfigure Scottish social life (and British society as a whole) have been obscured by a debate which merely poses the choice between separatism and unionism. For there are rich Scots, very rich Scots – and very poor Scots ... Ian Levitt draws attention to the marked inequalities in income which do not arise from differing skills, contributions to community life or needs. The top two per cent earn seven per cent of total income (more than half of that coming from unearned income in investments and profits), the top five per cent earn fifteen per cent of income and the top twelve per cent of Scottish people earn as much as the bottom fifty per cent ...

There are three distinguishing marks of the new structure of inequality in Scotland – the failure of taxation to erode the power of private property (those earning below £2,000 in 1971 paid half income tax), the dramatic growth of private occupational and pensions schemes to create a new structure of privilege within our social security system, and the sheer extent of poverty itself ...

Community Democracy

Scotland desperately needs a widely articulated and sufficiently popular concept of welfare and need grounded in equality and reciprocity in framing social policies and social priorities. Bryant, Cameron, Grant, Cook and Levitt all point to what is urgently required merely to meet people's elemental needs – a massive expansion in housing and community amenities, a regeneration of the public sector, and improvement of public health facilities especially in the community and industrial health fields, greater concentration of educational resources among those with the least opportunities, and a phasing out of means-tested benefits by adequate provision by right for the old, the single parent family, the unemployed, the disabled, and the low paid. But from community action groups – tenants associations, organisations of the unemployed, the old, the homeless, and the sick, movements to fight oil-related developments, anti-social planning decisions and so on – to the activities of specialised pressure groups and professional social workers, teachers and health workers themselves, the demand is increasingly that society be organised in a manner to cater for people's needs, that community goals be set to meet people's requirements as they express them. If the prospects for the least fortunate are to be as great as they can be, then they must have the final say – and that requires a massive and irreversible shift of power to working people, a framework of free universal welfare services controlled by the people who use them ... A first step could be compiling on a nation-wide basis an inventory of social needs, 'a social audit' prepared by community groups themselves. But socialism will have to be won also at the point of production – the production of needs, ideas and particularly of goods and services. And that demands ending the power of a minority through ownership and control to direct the energies of all other members of our society …

A Planned Economy

Niven argues that the public sector which employs 30 per cent of Scottish workers can be expanded in a manner which would dominate rather than respond to market requirements. Clearly the logic of present economic developments point in this direction. It is not just the demand of working people for a fuller share of the social product of their labour (and their collective power to resist the old formulas of unemployment and low wages in recession) – but also the cleft stick of labour-displacing technology. The more automation there is, the greater is the need to deal with the social consequences by increased public expenditure; yet the more the government raises taxation, the more urgent is the need for more automation. Thus, increasingly, the private control of industry has become a hindrance to the further unfolding of the social forces of production. Consequently, Michael Barratt Brown has convincingly argued that increased state intervention in social and economic affairs implies that it is no longer realistic to envisage a socialist commodity exchange market in a transition from capitalism to socialism, and as a corollary, that an ever advancing technologically-based economy is not the only way forward for underdeveloped regions or countries. Whether through investment in state owned industry in the central belt or through the application of intermediate technology, as Carter proposes, to the rural areas of Scotland, it is the erosion of the power of the market – and of the multinationals who now manipulate the market – to determine social priorities that is the forging ground for socialist progress.

The question of what socialist policies are required to meet the demands, skills and needs of Scottish working people raises the question of how the Scottish Labour Movement can force the pace of the advance towards socialism in Britain.

Certain definite points of advance are obvious at a British level, although this does not rule out socialists pressing for an economic control co-extensive with economic devolution under a Scottish Assembly: the public control of industries essential to the provision of social needs and services, the priorities being building and construction, food and food processing, insurance and pensions; the industries essential to the planning services vital to the economy – the priorities being energy as a whole, land, banking and foreign trade; industries whose monopolistic position threatens the ability of society to plan its own future – the priorities being the taking over of the assets of the major British and American multinationals in Scotland; and industries essential to regional development – in Scotland's case shipbuilding and textiles being the obvious cases.

Smith details what is required for the planned control of energy – the nationalisation of all offshore oil and gas industry, the private sector of BP, the British sector of Shell and the Burmah-Castrol Group, to become part of a National Hydrocarbons Authority, and of GEC to form the basis of a national nuclear corporation. But he also shows that if the benefits from oil are to be such that long term economic growth is possible then ICI should be taken over to form a public chemical corporation. The proceeds from oil could themselves be transferred into a regional development fund. A second basic area is land, vital to the future of Scotland, in providing food, timber and other services. Jim Sillars suggests a concrete plan for taking land into public ownership, John McEwen and Ian Carter in particular show what a socialist land strategy could involve and how industry suitable to the skills and needs of the local population and available resources could allow substantial local control over Highland development. Ray Burnett suggests that one obvious step could be an elected Highlands and Islands Development Board. A third area, investigated by Scott and Hughes, is the necessity for social control of the institutional investors who wield enormous financial power both in fostering privilege in our social security system and in controlling the economy. Two recent Labour Party pamphlets, 'Capital and Equality' and 'Banking and Insurance', propose how public control of banks, insurances and pensions companies could have a two-sided effect: creating greater social justice in the social services and providing substantial resources for industrial investment. Such a policy could be enacted without compensation and would in itself constitute a major erosion of the power of the British upper class. Public control to end the manipulative stranglehold of the monopolies would require a strategy to end the power of the British, American and European multinationals over the Scottish and British economies and in the event would require controls over foreign investment and trade, accepting a disengagement from a commitment to the free movement of capital in Europe. It would, as recent studies have indicated, require the forging of a new international economic framework based on long-term bilateral trading agreements for exchanges of goods and services and in the long run a payments union, possibly under the United Nations organisation, for clearing and extending such trade exchanges between nations, in particular, providing credit to underdeveloped countries.

Clearly, such a strategy is far more possible in Britain as a whole, given the substantial (and often underrated) industrial and financial assets of private companies. Britain has 140 of Europe's top 400 companies and the private sector has twice as much invested abroad as foreign companies and financiers hold in Britain.

Workers' Power

But the demand for the economy to be directed according to people's needs requires that the need for meaningful work be prioritised. That involves a new and creative relationship between work, education and leisure, which breaks down the existing division of mental and manual labour and the extension of self-management at the work place. What has often been cited as an irresoluble clash in socialist theory between regulating material production according to human needs and the principle of eliminating the exploitative domination of man over man can only be met through producers controlling the organisation of the production process. Thus it is precisely the surging forwards of demands by trade unionists for real control over the decisions affecting their livelihood that will be the point of departure for socialists. In his study of industrial democracy, Alex Ferry shows that the greater the influence workers have over their working lives locally, the greater will be the demand to reduce managerial prerogatives. Workers' control is impossible, he suggests, in a society which is not socialist – but controls developed in our present society which deny the logic of the market are the embryo of a future society. Clearly the proposals for workers' shareholdings (which would, at 1 per cent in all of shares yearly, take at least fifty years to mean anything) and for worker directorships, are inadequate. But the most outspoken proponent of workers' control in Britain, Ken Coates, has seen the recent TUC proposals for industrial democracy – a supervisory board with 50 per cent workers representation having the final say in major investment decisions, closures, redeployment, location of plant and so on – as 'a cautious step in the right direction'. The Labour MP for Motherwell has suggested that much more could be achieved if 'these representatives could by law be able to call for a ballot of employees as to whether they wish a scheme to be prepared for the conversion of the enterprise to workers' control'.

Co-ordination is clearly required of workers' activity in different industries and unions. The trade unions themselves, as Ferry suggests, must take increased steps to link the demand for better conditions of work and pay with the pressure for increased control. If they do not, they will be left behind by rank and file action, such as we saw in Scotland in the last three months of 1974. Co-ordination, to be effective, must clearly be coherent around certain demands which allow a systematic advance in industry and society. The proposals of the Institute for Workers' Control at the time of the Upper Clyde Shipbuilders (UCS) occupations have more relevance than ever in today's recession. A first condition set by trade unions in face of threatened unemployment would be that if the existing market is inadequate to support continuous production of ships, steel, textiles and so on, then the government should be bound to investigate the possibility of raising the whole level of international trade through state-guaranteed or negotiated trade exchanges. A second condition would be that if redundancies are inevitable, then government, locally or nationally, should organise alternative production to meet social needs – such as housing and community facilities – which private enterprise is failing to produce. An overriding condition would be that workers in such situations have the right to elect for control over their enterprises. Workers' control on an international scale is clearly an alternative to nationalism …

This requires from the Labour Movement in Scotland today a positive commitment to creating a socialist society, a coherent strategy with rhythm and modality to each reform to cancel the logic of capitalism and a programme of immediate aims which leads out of one social order into another. Such a social reorganization, a phased extension of public control under workers' self-management and the prioritising of social needs set by the communities themselves – if sustained and enlarged, would, in E. P. Thompson's words, lead to 'a crisis not of despair and disintegration, but a crisis in which the necessity for a peaceful revolutionary transition to an alternative socialist logic became daily more evident …'

The question is not how men and women can be fitted to the needs of the system – but how the system can be fitted to the needs of men and women …

Can Brown Change Labour's Direction?

Paul Rogers

The first month of the Gordon Brown administration in Britain was marked by a number of decisions that gave mixed signals on defence and security policy. Mr Brown faced an immediate crisis in the form of a double attempted car bombing in Central London followed by an actual attack at Glasgow Airport. The response from the new Home Secretary, Jacqui Smith, and from Mr Brown himself, was to focus on the incidents as examples of potential mass criminality rather than to emphasise terrorism. This was a marked change from the Blair government, especially the responses that had been typical from the combative former Home Secretary, Dr. John Reid. Even so, a series of decisions announced by the government at the end of the parliamentary session in July gave some mixed indications of the future direction of UK defence and security policy.

One of the most surprising was the decision to phase out the Defence Export Services Organisation (DESO), a government department that has promoted UK arms exports for 40 years. DESO's activities will be integrated into general trade support but the decision was welcomed by groups such as the Campaign Against the Arms Trade, which had long argued that it was anomalous that a government department should support private industry in this manner. The government's argument had previously been that DESO was a feature of an era when much of the British defence industry was nationalised, but substantive privatisation and recent controversies over alleged bribery and corruption involving arms deals in the Middle East had made it less easy for supporters to argue for the continuation of the Defence Export Services Organisation.

Missile Defence

Whereas the DESO phase-out suggested a change in outlook by the Brown administration, two other decisions indicated otherwise. One was the announcement that Britain would allow the United States to use its substantial facility at

Paul Rogers is Professor of Peace Studies at the University of Bradford. His latest book is entitled Global Security and the War on Terror *(Routledge).*

Menwith Hill in North Yorkshire to be part of the ballistic missile defence programme, the other being confirmation of a plan to build two very large aircraft carriers. Menwith Hill is a major signalling station that connects with a number of US surveillance and communications satellites, with one cluster of satellites specifically established to provide early tracking of offensive missiles. Britain also houses one of the ground stations in the Defence Early Warning System (DEWS) at Fylingdales, also in North Yorkshire, where a large phased array radar complex provides direct tracking data on missile flight paths. The two stations will together form a key part of the US missile defence system that is slowly taking shape.

Although the United States is extending its system to involve European states, with facilities planned in Poland and the Czech Republic, there are no current plans for interceptor missiles to be based in Britain. The scheme as it exists is about providing data for the defence of the United States alone, although that could change. The stated aim of the US system is to provide a substantial degree of protection against 'rogue states' such as Iran that might be capable, in a few years, of launching a small-scale missile attack on the United States. It involves the interception of incoming missiles when they are in the terminal phase of their flight path and is paralleled by other systems, including the planned deployment of the airborne laser, that would attempt to target missiles early in their flight when they are powered by their rocket motors and quite easily tracked by satellite-based infra-red detector systems. For almost every form of missile defence, such satellites are essential in giving an early indication of a missile launch, so Menwith Hill, as a key receiving station for such data, will be an integral part of the entire US missile defence programme.

From a US perspective an effective missile defence system is seen to add to the country's future security, but to states such as Russia and China it is a destabilising process that must be countered. From their perspective, if the United States becomes the only state able to maintain a large force of offensive nuclear-armed missiles and also has an effective defensive system, whereas they may not have the technical ability to develop workable defences and can only maintain offensive missiles, the United States will be seen as moving towards a destabilising advantage in any future balance of terror. The most obvious way to counter this is to produce more offensive missiles, at whatever the cost, in order to swamp any future US defence system. Russia is currently using some of its recently acquired economic muscle to revive its long-range nuclear missile programme and Chinese officials talk readily, if reluctantly, of the need for massive increases in their small force of long-range missiles to counter the US programme.

Such thinking may seem extraordinary but it is worth remembering that this was a major feature of Cold War nuclear strategy. Indeed the purpose of the 1972 Anti-Ballistic Missile Treaty (ABM) was precisely to prevent such an action-reaction process, limiting each side to protection of either its capital city or a single long-range missile field. Both the United States and the then Soviet Union built crude missile defences that were limited under the Treaty, but these were essentially ineffective. With the Bush administration having withdrawn from the Anti-Ballistic Missile Treaty, and with technological advances in the United States now making it more likely that missile defence becomes feasible, the risk is that the US programme, with British involvement, sets off a new arms race.

Aircraft Carriers

The second decision of the Brown government was to go ahead with a plan to order two huge new aircraft carriers. These ships, already named as *HMS Queen Elizabeth* and *HMS Prince of Wales,* will be very much larger than any warship to be deployed by the Royal Navy. At 65,000 tonnes each they will be substantially larger than the fleet carriers of the 1950s such as *HMS Eagle*, even larger than the battleship *HMS Vanguard*, and three times the size of the current *Invincible*-class aircraft carriers. They will be deployed with a new and massively expensive American aircraft, the F-35, and are due to be deployed in the mid-2010s, although it is not clear that the first of the F-35s will be ready for the British carriers by that time, given current development problems and cost over-runs.

The full life-time costs of the two new carriers together with the Trident nuclear missile replacement programme will be around £100 billion, and the end result will be to enable Britain to engage in large-scale expeditionary warfare, with a nuclear back-up, at a level which will not have been possible for forty years. The French are planning to build one such carrier and are actually sharing some of the design costs of the British ships, but their existing carrier, the nuclear-powered *Charles de Gaulle*, is a smaller ship and has been troubled with numerous problems ever since it was first deployed. The end result is that the UK carrier decision will mean that Britain will be the one country best able to deploy alongside the US Navy with its even larger *Nimitz*-class aircraft carriers.

There are two main problems with the carrier decision, especially when it is analysed alongside the earlier decision to replace the Trident missile submarines. The first is financial, given that the two programmes will together consume substantial parts of the Ministry of Defence's entire equipment budget. This is causing substantial unease in the British Army, with senior commanders complaining bitterly, if mostly in private, about how badly the Army is overstretched with its commitments in Iraq and Afghanistan. Army planners argue forcefully that Afghanistan is much more typical of the kind of conflict that Britain is likely to be involved in. It is not the kind of conflict that requires huge aircraft carriers, whereas amphibious capabilities and smaller carriers such as the *Invincible*-class may be rather more appropriate for a country the size of Britain.

Perhaps surprisingly, there is also substantial unease within the Royal Navy. The fears being expressed, again privately, are that the carrier/Trident replacement programmes are very much a case of all the eggs in two baskets. Furthermore, there are already indications that Royal Navy budgets are being squeezed. One example is that the full force of the Navy's new *Daring*-class destroyers is already very unlikely to be built. An even bigger issue for the Navy is that its amphibious warfare vessels, *HMS Albion* and *HMS Bulwark*, will both need replacing in about

20 years, with initial planning, design and development starting within a decade. The fear is that this will coincide with the huge costs of buying the F-35 and the peak expenditure on the next generation of ballistic missile submarines. Both will come at a time when the Army may be experiencing continuing stresses and the Royal Air Force will be wanting to replace its own white elephant, the Typhoon Eurofighter, and will be needing to acquire more heavy transport aircraft to support the Army.

What concerns the more far-sighted Navy planners is that they will end up losing one of their three main roles – carrier air power, the strategic nuclear role and the amphibious force – and it will be the latter that will disappear. Large aircraft carriers require a lot of support, in the form of destroyers, frigates and auxiliary vessels. At any one time it will only be possible to field one carrier task group. Similarly, the post-Trident missile force will be designed just to have one missile submarine available at any one time. In essence, in twenty or so years time, the Royal Navy will have the capability of putting just two capital ships to sea, not something some of the more thoughtful admirals are happy to contemplate.

What Kind of Security Policy?

The second problem with the carrier decision is much more broad. This is the way in which it moves the overall thrust of British defence policy in a particular direction – that of being able to mount large-scale expeditionary warfare alongside the United States. The unwritten assumption is that what lies behind the decision is that the key strategic region of the world during the lifetime of these new warships will be the Persian Gulf – host to almost two-thirds of the world's oil reserves and a substantial minority of the world's natural gas reserves. Britain is rapidly becoming a substantial oil importer, not on the scale of the United States and China, but still developing a vulnerability in energy supply that could prove uncomfortable. The United States is configuring much of its defence capability around maintaining the security of the Persian Gulf, and Britain's carrier programme will give it the capability to operate alongside the US Navy in the region. This may be seen as yet another example of maintaining a special relationship with the United States, but it also means that Britain will remain heavily committed to a view of the world that may simply be obsolete.

The really major security issues in the coming decades are much more likely to be the widening socio-economic divide and a global system that is coming up against environmental constraints on human activity. These are likely to come together over the issue of climate change, as the effects on the tropics make far more people desperate as they seek to survive violent and unpredictable weather and, especially, the probable drying out of many of the richest tropical croplands. Responding to the issues of the wealth-poverty divide and climate change requires major policy developments in trade, debt relief, assistance for sustainable development, and a curbing of carbon emissions that are far more radical than anything currently planned.

That alone will require a rapid move away from the current oil and gas dependency of countries such as Britain that would itself greatly diminish the strategic importance of the Persian Gulf. While the British government does profess a concern with issues of development and climate change, and government policy on the former has been significantly more positive in recent years, there appears to be no integrated thinking on the issues in terms of defence policy. In the context of what needs to be done to improve prospects for global security, the aircraft carrier and Trident replacement decisions are much more in line with a mode of thought that focuses on the 'control paradigm' of maintaining the status quo rather than addressing the likely causes of future insecurity.

An Indication of Ambivalence

What is interesting is that the Menwith Hill and aircraft carrier decisions appear to have been made when other parts of the Brown government are indicating potential changes in policy. The reaction to the London and Glasgow incidents is one example, and the more recent announcements of substantial government aid for community cohesion and what are described as moderate Islamic initiatives is another. It is also relevant that Mr Brown has appointed his own specialist on the Israel/Palestine issue, Michael Williams, in spite of Tony Blair taking on his own post-prime ministerial role.

Mr Brown's visit to Washington and New York at the end of July was also significant in that he was careful not to imply that the British presence in Iraq would be indefinite, he avoided the use of terms such as 'war on terror', sought to engage with Congress and, above all, delivered a powerful speech at the United Nations that focused primarily on issues of poverty and international development. On the basis of these developments it is certainly possible to argue that there is scope for a Brown administration to embrace ideas of sustainable security.

The main problem is that there appears to be a serious lack of integrated thinking across government, and this is compounded by two other issues. One is that Labour governments in Britain are traditionally concerned about being seen as weak on defence. This militates against their moving away from core aspects of defence policy such as the close security linkages with the United States and the nuclear issue. In practice it has tended to be Conservative governments that are willing and able to go in for defence budget cuts if economic circumstances demand. One of the ironies of the aircraft carrier decision is that the government of Margaret Thatcher was planning to sell one of the new *Invincible*-class carriers back in 1982, a decision only reversed by the outbreak of the Falklands-Malvinas War.

The second is that the Brown government inherited a defence posture in which the Trident replacement decision had already been made, and the carrier decision was imminent. It might have been wiser for the incoming government to put both decisions on hold pending a full re-evaluation of British security policy. This would have gone far beyond traditional defence reviews to consider precisely the kinds of major global trends that will most affect security in the coming decades. Such a review might still be possible, but it will certainly not be considered by a Brown government before a general election. From Labour's political perspective, and its history of being seen as weak on defence, a pre-election period is not the time for a fundamental reassessment of UK security policy. That is a really unfortunate matter of timing, but neither the Trident replacement nor the aircraft carrier decisions are set in stone. Given some of the other signals coming from the Brown government, it is certainly possible that a confident re-elected administration would be willing to engage in a considered response to the new global challenges. If so, it would be markedly different from the latter years of the Blair era.

With grateful acknowledgements to the Oxford Research Group (www.oxfordresearchgroup.org.uk).

Fighting for Trade Union freedom

Build peace not bombs - no new Trident

Bob Crow
General Secretary

John Leach
President

The Prospects for Labour

J.E. Mortimer

Jim Mortimer was General Secretary of the Labour Party from 1982 to 1985. He chairs the editorial board of Socialist Campaign Group News.

The prospects for the Labour Government under Gordon Brown depend not solely upon the convictions of one person, no matter how strongly he personally may seek to influence events, but on the response of the entire labour movement to the challenges that face Britain.

The propensity for favourable change under the leadership of Gordon Brown is better than it was under Tony Blair. Blair had very shallow roots in the labour movement and, to judge by many of his statements and actions, many of his convictions are far removed from those traditionally associated with organised labour. He appeared to prefer the profit motivation of the private sector to the public service ethos of the public sector. Hence his perpetuation of the policy of privatisation. He discarded the traditional policy of the labour movement on public sector housing at affordable rents for working people, built under local authority control and often with direct labour. He appeared to be indifferent to the growing inequality in British society. On education, to which he claimed he would give priority, he is remembered for further undermining the comprehensive principle, for the introduction of so-called academies with their wealthy sponsors, and for student fees. On trade union rights he failed to repeal some of the worst features of the anti-union legislation inherited from previous Tory governments. Under Tony Blair the British Government often argued in Europe for 'flexibility' as a means of avoiding the regulation of working conditions for the benefit of workers.

In international affairs Tony Blair is remembered as the most sycophantic supporter of one of the most reactionary Presidents in the history of the United States. The folly of this policy has been very costly. Hundreds of thousands of lives have been lost, principally citizens of Iraq, but also including British troops. Iraq has been reduced to violent chaos, and religious extremism has been given a boost in many countries as a response to the injustice of a war based on lies and deception.

It is important not to overlook that Gordon Brown was a member of the Blair administration throughout its period of office. He cannot escape his share of the responsibility for many of the policies pursued since 1997. On the other hand, within his own area of special responsibility, some measures were taken more in keeping with the traditions of the labour movement. He introduced tax changes designed to help the poorest in society. During his period of office as Chancellor of the Exchequer a relatively high level of employment was maintained, and there was economic growth. From his earlier writings it is clear that Gordon Brown had roots in the labour movement.

Future prospects do not, however, depend solely or even mainly on the personal differences of view between Tony Blair and Gordon Brown. Even more important will be the response of the labour movement and particularly the influence of the unions.

During recent years a new generation of trade union leaders have been elected. Predominately they are to the left of centre rather than to the right of centre. The trade union movement is not dominated by Blairites. These elections have been an indication of the thinking of the rank-and-file of the trade union movement.

Unfortunately, it cannot be claimed that this trend in the unions has had much influence on the Labour leadership. Indeed, in recent years the powers of the Labour Party conference have been significantly curtailed, yet it is at the conference and through the trade union representatives on the National Executive Committee of the Party that trade union influence has traditionally been exerted.

The plain fact is that the constitutional changes made by the Labour Party — which have helped to reduce trade union influence — would not have been possible if the unions had opposed them. The unions have, for the most part, gone along with the constitutional changes that have diminished their potential power to influence policy.

This is not simply a constitutional issue. It is above all a trade union and political issue affecting the whole direction of the labour movement. It is, of course, true that trade union membership is not much more than 50 per cent of what it was at its maximum a generation ago, but the unions are still the bedrock of the British labour movement. Some union leaders have spoken out with their criticisms, but they need to be joined by others.

Moreover there is plenty of evidence that public opinion, and particularly working-class opinion, is receptive to a radical message. The majority are not in favour of creeping privatisation. They believe that the gross inequality of British society is unjust. They are in favour of good public services. They want an expanded housing programme, with a substantial role for local authorities. They want better pensions for the elderly and, in particular, the restoration of the link between earnings and State pensions. They are in favour of the early withdrawal of British troops from Iraq and Afghanistan.

The first tentative signs of changes of policy have come from within the Brown administration. The vital necessity now and in the months ahead is for a clear and unambiguous call from the trade union movement for changes in direction on a range of issues affecting the welfare and security of working people. This would not harm the Labour Government. On the contrary, it would help it.

www.unitetheunion.org.uk
www.tgwu.org.uk

Fighting for peace and justice

DEREK SIMPSON AND **TONY WOODLEY**
Joint General Secretaries

T&G section

New Beginnings? Or Dark Days Ahead?

Joe Marino

Joe Marino is General Secretary of the Bakers, Food and Allied Workers' Union.

New Leader, new direction? That's the question many trade unionists have been asking over the last few months as Tony Blair's long goodbye meandered to a conclusion, and Gordon Brown's coronation came and went. Time, of course, will tell, but early signs are not encouraging. It seems there will be changes to the packaging but the content will not be much different as far as trade unionists will be concerned.

Of course, there will be relief that a more open form of government – dare we say, more democratic – will be practised. But it is content that counts, not presentation. We had all hoped that lesson had been learnt by now. There may well be intention to further democratise the monarchical basis of the British State, but we need to see the detail. In any event, the long grass is getting longer as we wait. Or is this a cunning plan to eliminate the Peers by outliving them?

What is deeply alarming is the embrace of business and the total disregard of workers' interests. So that arch opponent of the national minimum wage, Digby Jones, is given a government adviser's post, but representatives of low paid workers are shunned. Has he really changed from his 'the unions are irrelevant' phase? I doubt that, and now such a philosophy is welcomed into Government decision making. And not even the fig leaf of a token trade union baron to mask the charade! As an example of the way forward, that is not encouraging. There will not be many ex-CBI bosses canvassing and working for Labour at the next election, will there? Here, as he built his new big tent team, was an opportunity for Gordon Brown to at least signal his intention of listening to the interest of the working people of Britain. Instead, it – and they – are shunned. No attempt even to balance the interests of business and labour – quite the reverse, in fact.

The contest for the Deputy Leadership did begin a process of dialogue and discussion. The majority of the candidates had in common the need to restore trust and democracy, to reconnect with the Party base whilst reaching out in a positive way to those outside the Party. It would be a pity if this was not built on and expanded so that a rebuilding of trust in the political process can begin. That is sadly needed and Gordon Brown has a unique opportunity to lead in this process. The issues raised in that campaign need expanding and the campaign itself seen as a basis for development of working class policies.

No doubt there will be things that workers will be able to support in the 'new' government's programme – no one will argue, for example, with more affordable house-building (bet they will – the 'not in my back yard' brigade), but it is the real direction and commitment of government policy that will decide attitudes. Certainly, the 'interests' of the big builders need tackling if this is to be a success. And more powers need to be given to local councils (along with a strengthening of local democracy) so they can build for need, not for profit. The jury is still well and truly out in this area, though early signs are not promising.

But we have lived off scraps for too long. The litany of 'advantages' trundled out by New Labour Blairites and their apologists to divert criticism from fundamental demands of the labour movement were nothing more than a smoke screen to shift the focus away from the failures to deliver even on the weak slogan of 'fairness not favours'. Those holding their breath for the deliverance of the Warwick Agreement, for example, would today be in the Guinness Book of Records for such a feat.

Whilst many of us are critical of the democratic deficit in the European Union, there are still some advantages to be drawn. Without a doubt, it is easier to sack workers in Britain than in the rest of the EU. The Tories now propose to make it easier still. Employers who dismiss workers in the United Kingdom escape the social cost of their actions, whilst in other EU countries they are made to pay that cost. Here is a quick win for Gordon Brown – full implementation of the Social Chapter, with no opt out. Of course, big business will not tolerate that, so the Government won't even discuss it. They would, it seems, prefer to give the employers the freedom to sack at will. Whilst at the same time continuing to deny workers, via their unions, the right to organise against such actions, and to restrict severely the unions' ability to resist employer action by the use of draconian anti-labour laws. Instead of opposing John McDonnell's Trade Union Freedom Bill, we should be looking to a Brown Government to embrace it and promote it. Again, I fear we will be disappointed.

Internal Party democracy is an essential ingredient of any living labour organisation. For many it was the emasculation of Party democracy that led to the disillusionment with the Blairites and their programme. Iraq would have been impossible had the Labour Party had any vestige of internal democracy. Denied any avenue to vent their fury over such a débâcle, members chose to leave the Party – the only form of protest left to them. Not that this bothered the Blairites, who had no time for the Party, its members and affiliates in any event. Only foot soldiers at election time as far as they were concerned. So, in many ways, Gordon

Brown will be judged on the restoration of inner Party democracy. For a start, the right of Constituency Labour Parties and affiliated organisations to place on the Conference agenda issues of concern to them and to have them openly debated – rather than being shunted off to some Forum where they have little say and even less influence – is a must.

There needs to be a dynamic interplay between the Party and Unions, one built on respect and shared values. We are a long way from that – at least as far as ordinary union members are concerned – and a lot of work needs doing to rebuild that relationship. Of course, we will not get all we want – life is not like that. But, to be listened to with respect, to be given the same access as business, to have the party recognise there is a world outside the lobbyists and *Daily Mail,* will be a start.

We need to see a reconnection between the two wings of the labour movement and it is on progress in that reconnection that much will depend. Let us not forget that Gordon Brown was as much an architect of New Labour as was Tony Blair. If all we are to see is the same old policy only dressed in new clothes then there are dark days ahead. Unions need to use whatever influence they have in the Party to ensure a new direction from a new Government, one based on supportable policies that deliver the goods for working people and their families. As I said at the start – the jury is still well and truly out.

COMMUNICATION WORKERS UNION

End the occupation of Iraq and Afghanistan

No war on Iran

Billy Hayes
General Secretary

Jane Loftus
President

Kurt Vonnegut

A friend

Ralph Steadman

Facing page: Ralph Steadman's last drawing of Kurt Vonnegut on a table cloth, after lunch at his favourite restaurant in New York called Ristorante Lasagne. More of Ralph's work can be found online (www.ralphsteadman.com).

I hardly knew him. He appeared in my life like a rare butterfly. Why should I have known him? He was a writer and an American. I am an artist and Welsh. But in spite of that, we did meet – a mere five years ago – and still hardly struck up what people call a friendship. But then there was Joe Petro III, who knew us both. Joe is another artist and a printer of fine things. Joe made sure that we did meet and whether we wanted to or not, we were going to get on – because Joe said so. Kurt thought that Joe was God because Joe had somehow transformed us two into first cousins. It was a pretty neat trick.

Joe also printed for the both of us and Joe prints what is dear to both of us – our very own work.

That was how Kurt and I got friendly – very slowly – the best of possible ways. I had been aware of the huge legacy that is Kurt through his mass of writing – and especially his love of Mark Twain and Abraham Lincoln. One of Kurt's books is called BLUEBEARD, a story about Kurt and art, Kurt and his opinions of artists and his general philosophy of life and art. I knew instinctively that I would like him if I ever met him. I knew that what he really wanted to be was an artist and when I did meet him he had become one. He had more or less written all the words he would ever want to write. Kurt also knew particular heroes of mine like Saul Steinberg, the cartoonist, and Jackson Pollock the painter, expert dribbler and blotting master.

Kurt too became the best of artists, the kind who makes fearless marks on paper which mean what he wants them to mean. They are marks of intent and they are very much a shorthand way of reaching out and saying HI! to a complete stranger who just happens to have bought one of these marks as a print. Kurt's pride was that a complete stranger would actually hang one of these prints on their wall.

Meeting Kurt and getting to know him was both a delight and a journey of infinite possibilities. He enjoyed his food, his

'Manhattans' and his cigarettes. It was the cigarettes that were supposed to kill him. He tried hard with that in mind, but when they didn't kill him Kurt was going to sue the Tobacco Companies for making false claims on their packets that SMOKING KILLS. Instead he died in such a dumb-assed way by falling down the steep stone steps of his brownstone house on 48th street in New York. He lay in a coma for weeks and for those of us who knew, we wished him to wake up and reach out for his cigarettes, so that he could go on killing himself in his own way.

Kurt Vonnegut was uncomplicated, modest and so witty ... the second great writer I had known who fell off the landscape of my mind like a monumental cliff face. He never got to read the last letter I had sent him a week earlier and I can't remember now what it said.

scottish left review

Since 2000 the Scottish Left Review has been Scotland's leading journal of radical politics. It is non-party but aims to provide a space for ideas and debate for those on the Left of all parties and none.

Read current issues and subscribe at

www.scottishleftreview.org

My last word

Kurt Vonnegut interviewed by J. Rentilly

Kurt Vonnegut was once called 'the laughing prophet of doom'. While the description is somewhat apt, it doesn't come close to telling the whole story about the late author of *Slaughterhouse-Five* and recent bestseller *A Man Without a Country*, as well as 20 other books. A World War Two veteran and prisoner of war who survived the bombing of Dresden, Vonnegut was also a widely quoted social critic, an easily recognizable public figure (yes, that was Vonnegut in the Rodney Dangerfield campus comedy *Back to School*), and, in recent years, a prolific artist. Vonnegut's paintings, drawings, and sculpture – many of them inspired by themes or characters in his writings – are critically acclaimed and available for limited-edition purchase at kurtvonnegut.com.

All too often, Vonnegut was shoehorned into the 'science-fiction ghetto' – a sore underestimation of his witty, soulful, and wizened prose. But in his hometown of Indianapolis, 2007 marks a yearlong celebration of all things Vonnegut. Many readers and critics alike believe 'The Year of Vonnegut', produced by the Indianapolis-Marion County Public Library and the Indianapolis Cultural Development Commission, is a long time coming, and that Vonnegut – whose writings frequently intimate that time is merely illusory– is a treasure of the past, present, and future. 'I think these folks must be crazy', the author said about the acclaim, chasing the comment with an infectious, cigarette-charred laugh. 'But that's okay by me.'

Tell me the reasons you've been attracted to a life of creation, whether as a writer or an artist.

I've been drawing all my life, just as a hobby, without really having shows or anything. It's just an agreeable thing to do, and I recommend it to everybody. I always say to people, practise an art, no matter how well or badly you do it, because then you have the experience of

J. Rentilly, a journalist based in Los Angeles, interviewed Kurt Vonnegut for US Airways *magazine, shortly before his death in April 2007. We reprint the interview with grateful acknowledgements.*
J. Rentilly's remarks are in italic and Kurt Vonnegut's in ordinary type.

becoming, and it makes your soul grow. That includes singing, dancing, writing, drawing, playing a musical instrument. One thing I hate about school committees today is that they cut arts programs out of the curriculum because they say the arts aren't a way to make a living. Well, there are lots of things worth doing that are no way to make a living. [*Laughs.*] They are agreeable ways to make a more agreeable life.

I am having some success with paintings now because I'm well known. People would have no interest in them otherwise, and that's all right. I made them simply for the pleasure of creation. I speak with real painters and real artists from time to time about when they get their rocks off, and it's the process of actually doing it. The rest of it – rave reviews or flops, or whatever – is just noise to them. It's the doing that matters, the becoming. The rest of it doesn't really matter.

In the process of your becoming, you've given the world much warmth and humour. That matters, doesn't it?

I asked my son Mark what he thought life was all about, and he said, 'We are here to help each other get through this thing, whatever it is'. I think that says it best. You can do that as a comedian, a writer, a painter, a musician. He's a paediatrician. There are all kinds of ways we can help each other get through today. There are some things that help. Musicians really do it for me. I wish I were one, because they help a lot. They help us get through a couple hours.

When did the art become important to you, something you did regularly?

My grandfather, Bernard Vonnegut, was an Indianapolis architect and a painter. My father was an architect and a painter. My sister was a very good sculptress. So there were artists and art supplies around the house all the time. I could fart around as much as I wanted. I didn't take it seriously. I was as unserious as Jackson Pollock, throwing a canvas on the ground and messing it up in the most beautiful ways.

'A lack of seriousness', you wrote, 'has led to all sorts of wonderful insights'.

Yes. The world is too serious. To get mad at a work of art – because maybe somebody, somewhere is blowing his stack over what I've done – is like getting mad at a hot fudge sundae.

Nearly forty years after Slaughterhouse-Five, people still love reading your books. Why do you think your books have such enduring appeal?

I've said it before: I write in the voice of a child. That makes me readable in high school. [*Laughs.*] Not too many big sentences. But I hope that my ideas attract a lively dialogue, even if my sentences are simple. Simple sentences have always served me well. And I don't use semicolons. It's hard to read anyway, especially for high school kids. Also, I avoid irony. I don't like people saying one thing and meaning the other.

Do you feel we're living through an odd time in history, both nationally and globally?

Well, my late brother Bernie, who was a great expert on weather – at one point he knew more about tornadoes than anybody else on the planet, I imagine – was always approached by people who knew his background and wanted him to be an expert about it. 'Bernie, isn't this weather unusual?' And he would say, 'The weather is always unusual'. I mean, this is a very special time in history, but every time is.

When Timequake *was published ten years ago, you said you were basically retired as a writer. You've published two essay collections since then,* God Bless You, Dr. Kevorkian *and the best-selling* A Man Without a Country. *I wonder if the visual arts have become a substitute for writing in your life.*

Well, it's something to do in my old age. [*Laughs.*] As you may know, I'm suing a cigarette company because their product hasn't killed me yet.

Is it a different creative process for you, sitting down to write or picking up a paintbrush?

No. I used to teach a writer's workshop at the University of Iowa back in the '60s, and I would say at the start of every semester, 'The role model for this course is Vincent van Gogh – who sold two paintings to his brother'. [*Laughs.*] I just sit and wait to see what's inside me, and that's the case for writing or for drawing, and then out it comes. There are times when nothing comes. James Brooks, the fine abstract-expressionist, I asked him what painting was like for him, and he said, 'I put the first stroke on the canvas and then the canvas has to do half the work'. That's how serious painters are. They're waiting for the canvas to do half the work. [*Laughs.*] Come on. Wake up.

Your wife, Jill Krementz, is a superb photographer. I wonder if her work has had any influence or provided inspiration for you as an artist.

No. But it's been a pretty big part of the marriage. I fell in love with her talent. [*Laughs.*] I'm just so proud of her. As a consumer of her work, I like it so much, and she really knows what she's doing. She uses very little film. She just knows when to shoot. I asked her one time how she knew when to shoot. She told me about a photo session she was doing between a man and a woman [who were interested in] each other, and the moment to shoot was when the man ran out of material and no longer knew what to say. [*Laughs.*]

We live in a very visual world today. Do words have any power left?

I was at a symposium some years back with my friends Joseph Heller and William Styron, both dead now, and we were talking about the death of the novel and the death of poetry, and Styron pointed out that the novel has always been an élitist art form. It's an art form for very few people, because only a few can read very well. I've said that to open a novel is to arrive in a music hall and be handed a viola. You have to perform. [*Laughs.*] To stare at horizontal lines of phonetic symbols and Arabic numerals and to be able to put a show on in your head, it requires the reader to perform. If you can do it, you can go whaling in the South Pacific with Herman Melville, or you can watch Madame Bovary make a mess of her life in Paris. With pictures and movies, all you have to do is sit there and look at them and it happens to you.

Many years ago, you said that a writer's job is to use the time of a stranger in such a way that he or she will not feel the time was wasted. There are a lot of ways for a stranger to pass time these days.

That's right. There are all these other things to do with time. It used to be people would wonder what the hell they were going to do for the winter. [*Laughs.*] Then a big book would come out – a big, wonderful book – and everybody would be reading it to pass the time. It was a very primitive experiment, before television, where people would have to look at ink on paper, for God's sake. I myself grew up when radio was very important. I'd come home from school and turn on the radio. There were funny comedians and wonderful music, and there were plays. I used to pass time with radio. Now, you don't have to be literate to have a nice time.

You've stated that television is one of the most viable art forms in the world today.

Well, it is. It works like a dream. It's a way to hold attention, and it's awfully good at that. For a lot of people, TV is life itself. Churches used to provide people with better company than they had at home, but now, no matter what your neighbourhood life or family life is like, you turn on the television and you get relatives, family. I don't know if you've heard about this, but scientists have created baby geese that believe that an airplane is their mother. Human beings will believe in all kinds of things that aren't true, and that's okay. And TV is a part of that.

In your opinion, what's good on TV?

I have seen episodes of TV that would have been major Broadway plays in the '20s and '30s. That's where so much of our great writing is going on, [even] if very rarely. *Law & Order*, for example, deals with very subtle issues and social problems, very effectively and truthfully. That's one of the best things going, that show.

2007 has been dubbed 'The Year of Vonnegut'. When we spoke a few years back, you said that the acceptance of your community has always been important to you. Is this paradise found?

Well, paradise lost, really. We all should have extended families. We need them, just like we need vitamins and minerals. And most of us don't have those extended families anymore. I had one in Indianapolis, when I was born, which was in 1922. I had uncles and aunts all over the place, and cousins, family businesses that I could go into, whole rows of cottages that were full of my relatives. There was always someone to talk with, to play with, to learn from. I've lost all of that. They have been dispersed.

But the community, more generally speaking, is honouring you now – with celebrations and festivals. What do you make of that?

It's a very sweet honour. Of course, what it is, it's the idea of librarians there in Indianapolis – they have a great public library system, of which I was a great beneficiary when I was a kid – and it's a celebration of books and reading, really. Librarians, real heroes of our nation, have come forward to make this celebration, and that's a wonderful thing.

Is there another book in you, by chance?

No. Look, I'm 84 years old. Writers of fiction have usually done their best work by the time they're 45. Chess masters are through when they're 35, and so are baseball players. There are plenty of other people writing. Let them do it.

So what's the old man's game, then?

My country is in ruins. So I'm a fish in a poisoned fishbowl. I'm mostly just heartsick about this. There should have been hope. This should have been a great country. But we are despised all over the world now. I was hoping to build a country and add to its literature. That's why I served in World War Two, and that's why I wrote books.

When someone reads one of your books, what would you like them to take from the experience?

Well, I'd like the guy – or the girl, of course – to put the book down and think, 'This is the greatest man who ever lived.' [*Laughs.*]

The Socialist Aim

Jean Jaurès

The essay by Jean Jaurès, the French Socialist leader, from which this excerpt is taken, was published in Studies in Socialism *in 1906 by the Independent Labour Party. Spokesman Books are republishing this volume with a new introduction by Jim Mortimer (price £15). Order online at ww.spokesmanbooks.com*

The first condition of success for Socialism is that its essential characteristics should be explained clearly, so that everyone can understand them. There are many misunderstandings created by our adversaries, and some created by ourselves. We must do away with these.

The main idea of Socialism is simple and noble. The Socialists believe that the present form of property holding divides society into two great classes. One of these classes, the wage earning, the Proletariat, is obliged to pay to the other, the Capitalist, a sort of tax, in order to be able to live at all, and exercise its faculties to any degree. Here is a multitude of human beings, citizens; they possess nothing, they can live only by their work. But in order to work they need an expensive equipment which they have not got, and raw materials and capital which they have not got. Another class owns the means of production, the land, the factories, the machines, the raw materials, and accumulated capital in the form of money, and naturally this capitalist and possessing class, taking advantage of its power, makes the working and non-owning class pay a large forfeit. It does not rest content after it has been reimbursed for the advances it made and has repaired the wear and tear of the machinery. It levies in addition every year and indefinitely a considerable tax on the product of the workman and farmer, in the form of rent for farms, ground rent, rent of land in the cities, taxes for the payment of the public debt, industrial profit, commercial profit, and interest on stocks and bonds.

Therefore, in our present society, the work of the workers is not their exclusive property. And since, in our society founded on intensive production, economic activity is an essential function of every human being, as work forms an integral part of personality, the proletarian does not own his own body absolutely. The proletarian alienates a part of his activity, that is, a part of his being, for the profit of another class. The rights of man are incomplete and mutilated in him. He cannot perform a single act of his life without submitting to this restriction of his rights, this alienation of his very individuality. He has hardly left the factory, the mine, or the yard, where part of his effort has been expended in the creation of dividends and profits for the benefit of Capital, he has hardly gone back to the poor tenement where his family is huddled together, when he is face to face with another tax, other dues in the shape of rent. And besides this, State taxation in all its forms, direct taxation and indirect taxation, pares down his already twice diminished wage, and this not only to provide for the legitimate running expenses of a civilised society and for the advantage of all its members, but to guarantee the crushing payment of interest on the public debt for the profit of that same capitalist class, or for the maintenance of armaments at once formidable and useless. When, finally, the proletarian tries to buy, with the remnant of wages left to him after these inroads, the commodities which are necessities of daily life, he has two courses open to him. If he lacks time or money, he will turn to a retail dealer, and will then have to bear the expense of a cumbrous and unnecessary organisation of intermediary agents; or else he may go to a great store, where over and above the direct expenses of management and distribution he has to provide for the profit of ten or twelve per cent on the capital invested. Just as the old feudal road was blocked and cut up at every step by toll-rights and dues, so, for the proletarian, the road of life is cut by the feudal rights imposed upon him by Capital. He can neither work nor eat, clothe nor shelter himself without paying a sort of ransom to the owning and capitalist class.

And not only his life but his very liberty suffers by this system. If labour is to be really free, all the workers should be called upon to take part in the management of the work. They should have a share in the economic government of the shop, just as universal suffrage gives them a share in the political government of the city. Now, in the capitalist organisation of labour, the labourers play a passive role. They neither decide, nor do they help in deciding, what work shall be done nor in what direction available energies shall be employed. Without their consent, and often even without their knowledge, the capital which they have created undertakes or abandons this or that enterprise. They are the 'hands' of the capitalist system, only required to put into execution the schemes that capital alone has decided on. And the proletariat accomplishes these enterprises planned and willed by capital under the direction of chiefs selected by capital. So that the workers neither co-operate in determining the object of the work nor in regulating the mechanism of authority under which the work is performed. In other words, labour is doubly enslaved, since it is directed towards ends which it has not willed by means which it has not chosen. And so the same capitalist system which exploits the labour power of the workman restricts the liberty of the labourer. Thus the personality of the proletarian is lessened as well as his substance …

Jaurès

Leon Trotsky

Trotsky published his assessment of the French Socialist leader, Jean Jaurès, in a journal produced in Kiev in 1909.

Over modern French politics two figures loom: Clemenceau and Jaurès. It would not be at all difficult to explain how Clemenceau found at the bottom of his journalist's inkwell the means which permitted him finally to rule the destiny of France. This 'uncompromising' radical, this awesome toppler of ministries turned out in practice to be the last political resort of the French bourgeoisie: he 'ennobled' the rule of the stock exchange with the banner and phraseology of radicalism. In this case everything is clear to the last degree.

But what about Jaurès? What allows him to occupy so many places in the political life of the republic? The strength of his party? Of course, Jaurès would be inconceivable outside of his party; however, one cannot escape the impression, particularly if one is casting a glance from Germany, that Jaurès' role outgrew the real strength of his party. How do we explain this? By the might of his very individuality? But although personal charm might quite satisfactorily explain events within the limits of the drawing-room or the boudoir, on the political arena the most 'titanic' personalities remain the executive organs of social forces.

The solution to the riddle of Jaurès' political role lies in the *revolutionary tradition.*

What is tradition? The question is not as simple as it at first seems. Where does it nest: in material institutions? In one's individual consciousness? At first glance it seems to be in both places. But on examination it turns out to be somewhere deeper: in the sphere of the unconscious.

During a given period revolutionary events gripped France, saturated her air with its ideas, named her streets with its names and imprinted its triple slogans on the walls of her public buildings, from the Panthéon to the convict prisons. But then events, through the furious play of their inner forces, revealed their entire content and the last wave rose up high and fell back: reaction became enthroned. With a wicked indefatigability it exterminated all reminiscences of it from institutions, monuments, documents, from journalism, from everyday speech and what is even more striking, from social consciousness. Facts and names have been forgotten. Mysticism, eroticism and cynicism take the throne. Where are the revolutionary traditions? They have disappeared without trace ... But yet something imperceptible has happened, something has stirred, some unfamiliar draught has run through the atmosphere of France – the forgotten comes to life and the dead men rise up again. And traditions reveal all of their might. Where are they hiding? In the mysterious reservoirs of the unconscious somewhere at the extremities of the nerves that have undergone a historical processing which no decree can now repeal or abolish. Thus out of 1793 grew 1830, 1848 and 1871.

Imponderable and ethereal as these traditions are, they are however now becoming a real factor in politics for they are capable of becoming incarnate. Even in the worst days of its fallen spirit the French proletariat, torn to pieces in factions and sects, stood like a warning shadow over the official leaders of the fatherland. That is why the immediate political influence of the French workers has always been higher than their level of organization and their parliamentary representation. And it is in this historical force, which goes on from generation to generation, that Jaurès is strong.

But this Jaurès, the bearer of a heritage, is still not the whole Jaurès. He presents another side towards us, that of a parliamentarian of the Third Republic. A parliamentarian from top to toe! His world is that of the electoral pact, the parliamentary platform, the challenging question, the oratorical duel, the backstage agreement and, at times, the ambiguous compromise ... A compromise against which traditions and objectives alike – the past and the future – might be quick to protest. Where is the psychological knot which ties these two faces together?

'The practical man,' says Renan in his article on Cousin, 'has to be base. If he has lofty goals they will only mislead him. It is for this reason that great people take part in practical life only through their shortcomings and petty qualities.' In these words of a contemplative sceptic and spiritual Epicurean it is not hard to find they key to Jaurès contradictions: assuming that here we have not a malicious slander on man in general but on Jaurès in particular. All of life is practice, creation and doing. 'Lofty goals' cannot mislead for they are merely its organs, and practice will always maintain its supreme control over them. To say that practical man, i.e. *social man*, must be for the most part base means simply to expose one's own moral cynicism, to fear its practical conclusions and to immerse oneself in idealistic speculations.

Jaurès destroys Renan's slander on man by his whole moral stature. An impatient active idealism guides him in even his most foolhardy moves.

In the darkest days of Millerandism – 1902 – I had occasion to see Jaurès next to Millerand on the platform, hand in hand, apparently linked in a complete unity of aims and resource. But an unmistakable feeling told me that an unbridgeable abyss separated them: this extreme enthusiast, selfless and ardent, from that parliamentary careerist, cold and calculating. There is something overwhelmingly convincing, a sort of infantile athletic sincerity in his figure, his voice and his gestures ...

On the platform he seems huge and yet he is below average height. Thick-set, with a head sitting squarely on his neck, with expressive 'dancing' cheekbones, nostrils which swell up as he speaks wholly releasing the stream of his passion, he in appearance too belongs to the same human type as Mirabeau and Danton. As an orator he is incomparable and has met no comparison. There is not that finished and at time irritating refinement in his speech with which Vandervelde shines. He cannot be compared with Bebel for a logical force of attraction. The cruel and venomous irony of Victor Adler is foreign to him. But in spirit, in passion and in his verve he is the equal of them all ...

It is true that another thoroughbred Russian discovered in Jaurès merely a skilful technical erudition and pseudo-classical declamation. But what speaks in such an appraisal is nothing more than the poverty of our native culture. The French have an oratorical technique, a common heritage which they adopt without effort, and outside of which they are as inconceivable as a 'respectable' man without formal dress. Every speaking Frenchman speaks well. Hence the harder it is for a Frenchman to be a great orator. But Jaurès was just such. It is not his rich technique nor his enormous miraculous sounding voice nor the generous profuseness of his gestures but the *genius's naïveté of his enthusiasm* which brings Jaurés close to the masses and makes him what he is ...

But we have digressed from our question: what is the psychological knot which ties up in Jaurès an inheritor of Promethean traditions with a parliamentary operator?

What is Jaurès? An opportunist? Or a revolutionary? Both the one and the other depending on the political moment; and moreover he is ready to go to the ultimate extremes in either direction. Jaurès is a figure of *action*. He is always prepared to 'crown the thought with the crown of execution' ... During the Dreyfus Case Jaurès said to himself: 'whoever does not seize the executioner's hand poised over his victim will himself become the executioner's accomplice', and without pondering the political outcome of the campaign he threw himself into the flood of Dreyfusism. His teacher, friend and subsequent irreconcilable antagonist, Guesde, told him: 'Jaurès, I like you because your deed always follows on your thought!'

Herein lies the strength and the weakness of Jaurès.

'Any age believes,' wrote Heine, 'that its own struggle is more important than that of all the rest. It is in this that the faith of an age consists and it is in this faith that it lives and dies ...'

In Jaurès there is something beyond this religion of his age: he has the élan of the *moment*. He does not measure the transient political alignments against the great yardstick of historical perspectives. He is wholly and completely here amid the evil of the hour. And in serving the hour he is not afraid of coming into conflict with his higher aim. He expends his passion, energy and talent with such a spontaneous extravagance as if the outcome of the great struggle of the two worlds depended on each political question taken one by one.

In this strength of Jaurés lies, too, his fatal weakness. His politics lack proportion and frequently he cannot see the wood for the trees.

> *There is a tide in the affairs of men (says Shakespeare's Brutus)*
> *Which, taken at the flood, leads on to fortune;*
> *Omitted, all the voyage of their life*
> *Is bound in shallows and in miseries.*

In the mould and the scale of his character Jaurés was born for the epoch of the great flood. But he was fated to develop his talent in the period of grave European reaction. This is not his fault but his misfortune. But this misfortune in turn engendered his fault. Among his gifts Jaurés lacks one: the ability to *wait*. Not to wait sitting idly by, but to gather one's forces and prepare the tackle confidently reckoning on the approaching tempest. He wants immediately to switch over to the jangling coinage of practical success, to the great traditions and the great opportunities. From there he falls so often into insoluble contradictions 'in shallows and in miseries' of the Third Republic ...

Only a blind man would number Jaurés among the doctrinaires of political compromise. To such politics he has merely added his talents, his passion and his ability to go through to the end but he has not made a catechism out of it. And in the event Jairés will be the first to unfurl his mainsail and move off the shallows out to the open sea ...

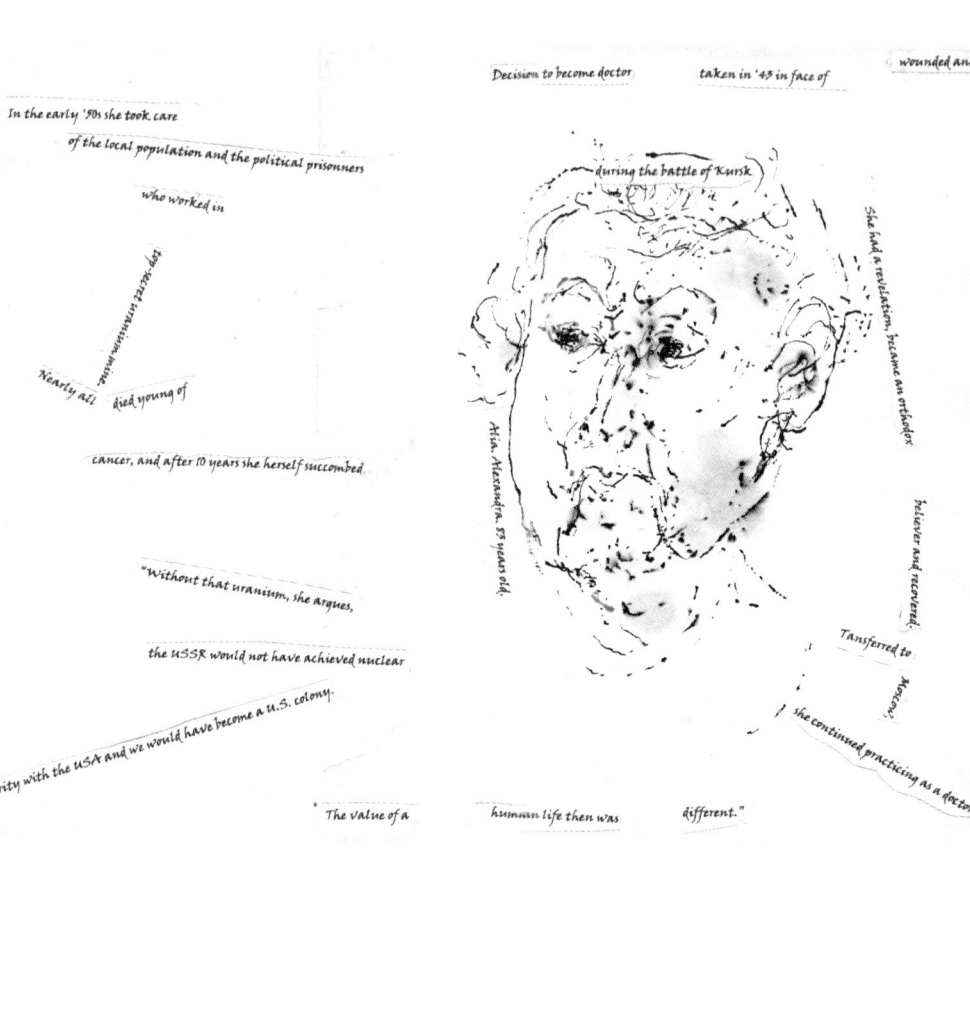

In the early '50s she took care of the local population and the political prisoners who worked in top-secret uranium mines. Nearly all died young of cancer, and after 10 years she herself succumbed.

"Without that uranium, she argues, the USSR would not have achieved nuclear parity with the USA and we would have become a U.S. colony.

Decision to become doctor taken in '43 in face of wounded and die during the battle of Kursk.

Atia Alexandra, 85 years old.

She had a revelation, became an orthodox believer and recovered. Transferred to Moscow, she continued practicing as a doctor.

"The value of a human life then was different."

Erasing the Past

John Berger

Facing page: John Berger's portrait of Alexandra, the doctor from Kursk. His latest books are Here is Where We Meet *(Bloomsbury, 2005),* Hold Everything Dear *(Verso, 2007) and* The Red Tenda of Bologna *(Drawbridge Books, 2007). More information about* The Drawbridge*, an exciting new journal, is available online (www.thedrawbridge.org.uk).*

Appearances like words can also be read and, amongst appearances, the human face constitutes one of the longest texts.

Alexandra visited Paris for the first time in her life – she's 83 – this spring. Until a couple of years ago she practised medicine in Moscow. She was born in Kursk, 800km to the south of the capital. Thanks to Russian friends I met her and the four of us had supper together at a table in a suburban garden towards the south of Paris.

I asked her what had made her decide to study medicine. The countless dying and wounded during the battle of Kursk, she replied. It was this battle, following Stalingrad, which directly opened the way for the Red Army's advance towards Berlin. The conversation in the garden continued slowly. She looks considerably younger than she is, and she has a way of talking which is aerial, casual and, at the same time, considered. The light faded, we brought out candles. Listening to her could bring you to Heidegger's insight that 'language is the house of being'; she makes you at home in this house.

When she qualified as a doctor in the 1950s, she was immediately dispatched to a uranium mine in Turkmenistan. The miners were *zeks*, political prisoners, from the Gulag. The USSR at that time urgently needed uranium to make its bombs, and thus to achieve nuclear parity with the USA and establish the 'mutual deterrence' that lasted until 1989.

After a few years nearly all the uranium miners foreseeably succumbed to cancer. As I did, said Alexandra. I prayed and I recovered and I returned to Moscow where I practised for a further forty years as a paediatrician.

Whilst she spoke, ate and laughed in the garden.

How do you explain your energy?

People! It's simple, I love people.

I had an insistent urge to draw her. I caught her eye and she nodded.

Before she rose to leave, I asked her to

choose between the two drawings I'd made. She chose the weaker of the two. I think deliberately; she wanted me to keep the firmer one.

* * *

The same week in the international press there was a photo of Bernard Kon, a 97-year-old Polish engineer living in Warsaw, who risked – according to a proposed new law – to lose his small state pension because he had volunteered in 1937 for the International Brigade and fought for the Republicans in the Spanish Civil War.

The expression of his eyes has something in common with that in Alexandra's eyes. Perhaps because the two of them saw some of the same things. Side by side their faces speak of personal achievements (and pain) which do not need to be acknowledged, for both of them, in their different ways, exude a sense, in part tragic and in part triumphant, of having chosen to tend to, and to pay attention to history, and thus to belong to it. And, strangely, it is this belonging that allows each of them to have such a distinct identity.

Fortunately the new law which threatened Bernard Kon and thousands of others is being declared unconstitutional, but the wiping-out-communism operation of the twin scarecrows Lech and Jaroslaw Kaczynski (President and then Prime Minister of Poland) continues, and is typical of many political initiatives today.

In choosing not to read the complex experiences of history, the ubiquitous aim of such initiatives is to erase the past, and thus to reduce all political choices to what is on instant display.

To put it graphically, the long text of the human face is being reduced to a mug shot.

* * *

If we had not mined the uranium to manufacture nuclear weapons, Alexandra said in the garden, we would have become an American colony.

The drawing of Alexandra was still on the table when I was reading the proofs of Naomi Klein's inestimably important book *The Shock Doctrine: The Rise of Disaster Capitalism**. In it she studies the career of the notorious economist Milton Friedman. Considered as a theorist, Friedman is somewhat reminiscent of Dr. Strangelove: a story of dogmatism, innocence, cynicism and a dream of being seen as a saviour. (He got a Nobel Prize.) He claimed that undistorted, 'pure' economies could settle everything. He has the face of a smiley uncle, who has never, never been out of doors, and who takes you to the window to explain what is and is not important in life.

He was also, however, a practical politician whose record is ruthless. He recognized from the beginning that his 'pure' solution to the human predicament would never be accepted by those on whom it was imposed, unless they were in a state of dire shock.

For people to go along with the dismemberment of social aid, the abolition of a minimal wage and of any control over working conditions, the privatization of social services, equal taxes for rich and poor, the loss of any legal right to effective

---

*Pubished by Penguin Books, £25

protest, for people to accept this deal (the polar opposite of Roosevelt's New Deal), they had first to suffer economic disaster and become panic-stricken.

This is the 'shock doctrine' which, for some time, has permeated and determined the global decisions of the G8, the World Bank, the IMF, the strategists of the CIA and – occasionally – the US Armed Forces. Sometimes the shock is totally engineered as in Chile (1973); sometimes it is opportunistically appropriated, as in Russia (1991) or South Africa (1996).

The startling revelation of Klein's book is that those who advocate and instigate Friedman's 'economic shock' were and are closely associated with the CIA teams (see the Kubark manual) working on techniques of coercive cross-questioning under physical shock – that's to say torturing prisoners.

One month before he was assassinated, my friend Orlando Letelier, Allende's Minister of Defence, made exactly the same connection between what was happening to the Chilean economy and to his comrades in prison. Orlando had the face of a singer for whom every song might be the last.

The two types of shock are different and they devastate in different ways. One is solitary and physical: the other collective and ontological. The first is mercilessly produced by electroshocks (assiduously studied by the CIA since the 1950s) and sensory deprivation. The second is produced by supervising and stage-managing an economic collapse, dismantling every previous social infrastructure, carefully timing a period of abject poverty and panic, and then cynically stepping forward with false promises. Both types of shock are applied in order to smash resistance, and this is done by first destroying the subject's sense of identity.

Those who administer the shocks – be they torturers, economists or scarecrows – have learnt, after fifty years of experiment, that the most effective way of destroying people's sense of identity is to systematically dismantle and fragment the story they have so far told themselves about their own lives, to erase the past.

The past once erased, any variant of a slogan which, despite its pretended innocence, is politically corrupt, may be used: Clean Break. Fresh Start. New Beginning. Such is the demagogy of neo-liberalism.

* * *

Alexandra was sitting in the garden during the French presidential election campaign. The style of the two principal candidates was remarkable for its rejection of explanations. Neither explained what is happening in the world, the impact of those happenings on France, or what the foreseeable consequences and, therefore, choices are likely to be. Both were mapless. And they were mapless because they did not dare to speak about history.

Such a conspiracy of silence changes profoundly the nature of an election. The first democratic principle is that the elected remain accountable to those who elected them: how they govern will later be assessed by those they govern. To put it differently: the elector's questioning of the elected has, in the long term, a role in the process of decision making. A dialectic of argument replaces blind, undemocratic obedience.

If candidates do not outline their vision of the epoch they're living in and lay out their proposed strategy for survival, if this remains unsaid and unread, the electorate cannot fulfil their dialectical role, for there has been no dialogue about the essentials. When a candidate is, or pretends to be, mapless, the electorate is reduced to being a dray-horse.

What I call a reading of history implies a shared taking into consideration of events, their causes and their consequences, a discussion about the possible margins of manoeuvre (history is seldom generous), and then the presentation and explanation of a policy. Promises made without this are all delinquent.

I suspect President Sarkozy because he has the economic shock doctrine up his sleeve.

Fifty years ago, Alexandra said, the value of human life was different.

I look again at Alexandra's face as she sat in the garden and I recall a sentence by Anton Chekhov, who was also a doctor. 'The role of the writer is to describe a situation so truthfully … that the reader can no longer evade it.' We today with our lived historical experiences, which the political machines are trying to erase, have to be both that reader and writer … it's within our power.

With grateful acknowledgements to The Drawbridge (www.thedrawbridge.org.uk).

Race & Class is a quarterly journal on racism, empire and globalisation, published by the Institute of Race Relations, London.

www.irr.org.uk

Recent highlights: *A. Sivanandan* on racism and the 'war on terror', *Liz Fekete* on enlightened fundamentalism, *Matt Carr* on Eurabia, *John Berger* on Palestine, *Anis Shivani* on the new Orientalism and *Avery F. Gordon* on Abu Ghraib and US prisons.

Individual issues cost £7. Subscriptions for individuals are £26 per year (4 issues). To subscribe or purchase an issue, phone 020 7837 0041, email info@irr.org.uk or write, enclosing a cheque, to IRR, 2–6 Leeke Street, London WC1X 9HS, UK.

American foreign policy at point zero

Gabriel Kolko

Gabriel Kolko's notable analyses of American foreign policy include Anatomy of a War; Vietnam, the United States, and the Modern Historical Experience *(New Press, 1985). His recent books include* The Age of War *(Lynne Rienner Publishers).*

The United States has rarely lost any conventional military battle since at least 1950. Nor has it, at the same time, ever won a war. It has successfully overthrown governments through interventions or subversion but the political results of all its efforts – as in Afghanistan in the 1980s and Iran in 1953 – have often made its subsequent geopolitical position far, far more tenuous. In a word, in international affairs it bumbles very badly and it has made an already highly unstable world far more precarious than it otherwise would be if only the US had left the world alone. No less important, Americans would be far better off thereby. Because – to repeat a critical point – it has failed to attain victory in any of the real wars it has fought since Korea. Its adversaries learned as long ago as the Korean War that decentralization would stymie America's overwhelming firepower, which was designed for concentrated armies, and provided a successful antidote for massive, expensive technology.

All this is very well known. The real issue is why the United States makes the identical mistakes over and over again and never learns from its errors.

At the present time it is losing two wars and creating a vast arc of profound strategic and political instability from the Mediterranean Sea to South Asia, it has resumed the arms race in Europe, and it is making Russia an enemy when it could easily have been friendly. Economically, it has run up the biggest deficits in American history, brought on the decline of the dollar, and wherever one turns this administration has been at least as bad as any in two centuries of American history – perhaps even the worst. We now have an unprecedented disaster in the conduct of American power, both overseas and at home, in part because of the people who now rule – ambitious men and women who calculate only what is best for their careers – but also because the imperatives and inexorable logic of past policies and conventional wisdom have brought us to this critical juncture. All the old mistakes have been repeated; nothing had been learned from the past, and official myopia is timeless.

A large part of the United States' problem, whether Republicans or Democrats are in power, is that it believes it has the right and obligation to intervene everywhere, in whatever forms they choose, and that its interests are global. Interventionism – so the consensus among Republicans and Democrats goes – is the cost of its global interests and mission, because it has been convinced for almost a century that it was preordained to remedy the world's many wrongs – and to do so by whatever means it chooses. There is nothing whatever that is unique in this regard in the present Bush Administration. This pretension, which first began during the nineteenth century and which Woodrow Wilson articulated, is simply not functional, and it has led to countless morasses, bad for the United States and far worse for the countries it has interfered with. The fact is that no nation has ever been able to assume such an international role, and those that have attempted to do so came to no good end – they exhausted their resources and passions and follies.

Political conflicts are not solved by military interventions, and that they are often incapable of being resolved by political or peaceful means does not alter the fact that force is dysfunctional. This is truer today than ever with the spread of weapons technology. The United States is not exempt from the facts that have guided international affairs for centuries.

The US has already lost the wars in Iraq and Afghanistan for the very same reasons it lost all of its earlier conflicts. It has the manpower and firepower advantage, as always, but these are ultimately irrelevant in the medium and long run. They were irrelevant in many contexts in which the United States was not involved, and they explain the outcome of many armed struggles over the past century regardless of who was in them, for they are usually decided by the socio-economic and political strength of the various sides – China after 1947 and Vietnam after 1972 are two examples but scarcely the only ones. It is a transcendent truism of global politics that wars are more determined by socio-economic and political factors than any other, and this was true long before the United States attempted to regulate the world's affairs.

But why?

All this still begs the issue of why the United States repeatedly makes the same drastic errors. Are there vested interests in preparing for war? Are illusions based on them, or ideologies – or both?

In part, expensive equipment and the incredibly inflated military budget are premised on the traditional assumption that owning complex weapons gives America power, which is determined by arms in hand rather than what happens in a nation's politics and society. In fact, the reverse is often the case, especially when enemies find the weaknesses in this sort of technology and exploit it – as they increasingly have done over the past decades. Then the cost of fighting wars becomes a liability – and America's technological military an immense weakness when the government has huge deficits or lacks funds to repair its ageing public infrastructure – a fact that was highlighted when the collapse of a bridge in

Minneapolis earlier this year led to the striking revelation that 70,000 bridges in the United States are rated deficient. The Vietnam War should have resolved the issue of the relevance of technology to America's military ambitions, but it did not. The real question is: why?

To a critical but scarcely exclusive sense, the Pentagon's penchant for military toys makes an ambitious, aggressive foreign policy essential. Without enemies and conflicts, real or potential, there is no reason to spend money, and this reality often coloured its definition of Soviet goals after 1947 – despite the objections of senior CIA analysts. But the Defense Department, and national security establishments in general, are immense and all kinds of constituencies exist in them: there are procurement experts who draw up budgets and go after equipment mindlessly, people who have always dominated its actions, but thinkers, too. Each does their own thing and they are often very different. It has always had these contradictions.

But that those who run the military establishment have technological illusions, which many ordinary people share in this and other domains of human existence, keeps immense sums of money flowing to arms manufacturers and their minions. There is a very profound consensus between the two parties on arms spending, which began under the Democrats a half-century ago and it will not go away – no matter how neglected the bridges and infrastructure, health, or the like. Arms lobbies are not only very powerful in Washington but create crucial jobs in most states, and military spending keeps the economy afloat. Weapons producers make money regardless of whether the Pentagon wins or loses its wars – and making money is their only objective. It is surely a key causal factor even if it is far from being the sole explanation of why the United States intervenes where it shouldn't.

It is close to impossible to assign some weight or priority to the arms industry, but it must be taken into account that the arms manufacturers have power. Strategic lobbies in Washington contribute heavily to politicians who need campaign funding, and gain financially whether America wins or loses it wars. They are the 'x-factor' in the equation but scarcely the sole one. But, at the least, they are very important even when not decisive.

Another explanation is ambitious politicians, who will say and do whatever is required to stay in power or gain it. This factor is so familiar that it scarcely requires repeating, but the cynical ways politicians treat polls and American public opinion is a crucial aspect of this question. There are indeed problems with the public but it invariably senses realities and their constraints well before the politicians – who use the public and then ignore it. The party out of office will cater to mass opinion but usually forgets it once it comes to power – as the recent Democratic Party trajectory shows. This is usually the rule but public opinion is an element that cannot be merely gainsaid, and as the Korean and Vietnam wars proved, it could play a decisive role. An increasing majority of the people think the war in Iraq is not worth fighting, and the President is among the most unpopular in history. The public may be impotent or far too passive for its own good, and generally is, but it is far less brainwashed than the advocates of 'manufactured consent' concede. How, when, or if its role becomes more crucial is a matter of conjecture. Its influence is usually negligible and takes far too much time to have an impact. Follies are committed long after the public condones them. But that it eventually becomes critical is a fact of life which one cannot make too much of, or too little.

Consensus on ideology and goals is crucial also, but that policies fail to work and are increasingly dangerous as a guide to action has been true for a long time and is more obvious as years elapse. The Bush Administration encapsulates it but the basic problem has existed for many decades. What the Bush coterie has seen is the culmination of a logic that is much older. It presides over a catastrophe that began many years ago.

All in all, these factors have delivered us to our present mess, which may very well exceed any in American history.

Some of the most acute criticisms made of the gross simplisms which have guided interventionist policies were produced within the military, especially after the Vietnam experience traumatized it. My history of the Vietnam War was purchased by many base libraries, and the military journals treated it in detail and very respectfully. The statement at the end of July by the new chairman of the Joint Chiefs of Staff, Admiral Michael G. Mullen, that 'no amount of troops in no amount of time will make much of a difference' if Iraqi politics fails to change drastically reflects a current of realism that has existed among military thinkers for some decades. (Whether he acts on this assumption is another matter and depends greatly on considerations outside of his control.) Like the CIA, the military has acute strategic thinkers, and the monographs of the US Army's Strategic Studies Institute – to name one of many – are often very insightful and critical. Academics tend to be irrelevant and dull by comparison.

The problem, of course, is that few (if any) at the decisive levels pay any attention to the critical ruminations that the military and CIA consistently produce. There is no shortage of insight among US official analysts – the problem that policy is rarely formulated with objective knowledge is a constraint on it. Ambitious people, who exist in ample quantity, say what their superiors wish to hear and rarely, if ever, contradict them. Iraq is but an example, for the entire mess there was predicted. If reason and clarity prevailed, America's role in the world would be utterly different.

Those in power simply ignore the critical military's insights, and the vast bulk of officers obey orders. Many of them know better. They have learned the hard way – experience. Neocon intellectuals and scribblers utterly lack it.

We are at point zero in the application of American power in the world: the United States cannot win its extremely expensive adventures, nor will it abstain from policies which increasingly lead to disasters for the nations in which it intervenes and for itself as well. All the factors I have mentioned – its myopia regarding technology, the policy consensus that binds ambitious politicians and often makes public opinion irrelevant, the arms makers and their local interests, or the limits of rational inputs – have all combined to deliver us to this impasse. It is difficult not to be pessimistic when – as it should be – realism rather than illusions guide our political assessments. But realism is the only way to avoid cynicism.

Blackwater

Kevin Cahill

Kevin Cahill is a journalist and author of standard reference works including Who Owns Britain and Ireland *and* Who Owns the World.

When the Iraq war crimes tribunals start, as start they must, the earliest defendants in the dock will surely be the Blackwater company and its hired mercenaries. And, as a shield for their murderous acts, they will no doubt carry before them the infamous Order 17. This was the reckless immunity granted to the private armies in Iraq by the ill-starred US 'administrator of Iraq', Paul Bremer III, in June 2004, the month he fled the country. In effect, Bremer placed the mercenary armies recruited by the Allies, and said to total over 180,000 personnel, beyond the reach of both Iraqi and the domestic law of their home countries, mainly the United States. In his book, Jeremy Scahill chronicles the consequences of privatising a modern war: *Blackwater, The rise of the world's most powerful mercenary army.**

In a book that is uniquely timely in its publication, Scahill, a journalist, charts the coming into existence and deployment in Iraq of a mercenary force from the United States, called Blackwater Inc. Timely, because shortly after the book's appearance in both the United States and the United Kingdom, in mid 2007, a force of Blackwater personnel fired on a crowd in Baghdad, killing between 11 and 17 people and wounding 23 others, on 20 September 2007. An outraged Iraqi Prime Minister, Nouri al Maliki, not famous for his criticism of the Americans, said of the incident that; 'We will not tolerate the killing of our citizens in cold blood', having earlier described the companies report on the incident as 'not accurate'. A Blackwater spokesperson, Anne E Tyrell, later told the *New York Times* that 'Blackwater's independent contractors acted lawfully and appropriately in response to a hostile attack in Baghdad on Sunday'. She described the people killed as 'armed insurgents'. In an account of the incident by the Iraqi police, an account that is now being indirectly accepted as accurate by the US State

---
*Published by Serpent's Tail, £12.99

Department, Blackwater's employer, the first three 'armed insurgents' killed were a man and his wife and their infant child. Maliki described the incident as 'the seventh of its kind "recently"'. The 'recently' got lost in translation because in the period covered by Scahill's book, from mid 2003 to the end of 2006, there were endless shooting incidents in which the Blackwater company and its staff were involved. Of these, one is appalling in its direct irresponsibility, and another appalling in its consequences.

The first incident, all too vividly described by Scahill, occurred at the holy city of Najaf on the 4th of April 2004. A group of Blackwater contractors, about eight in number, were guarding a local building occupied by Bremer's Coalition Provisional Authority. They were on the roof where a US marine corporal was installing communications equipment. A small riot or demonstration began in the square in front of the building. The Blackwater contractors subsequently took control of the action, of which the following are excerpts from the various accounts compiled by Scahill.

> 'The shooting stops as the men assess the situation below them. "Hold what you got. Hold what you got right there" a voice commands. "Just scan your sectors. Scan your sectors. Who needs ammo?"
> "Fuckin' niggers" says another voice as the men begin to reload their weapons'

All this was recorded on video and published on the web by a Blackwater contractor using a video camera in between killing Iraqis.

Later, the marine communications corporal, who was injured, is reported saying:

> 'I gazed over the streets with straining eyes, only to see hundreds of Iraqis lying all over the ground.' And he added, 'It was an unbelievable sight; even though there were so many lying dead, the Iraqis were still running towards the front gate. I opened fire once again. Emptying magazine after magazine, I watched the people dressed in white and black robes drop to the ground as my sights passed by them.'

And how did he feel about this mass slaughter?

> 'I had a weird feeling come over me' Young recalled. 'I had many emotions kick in at once. I felt a sense of purpose, happiness, and sorrow, which all hit me at once.'

The point Scahill makes about this action, in which an uncounted number of Iraqis were killed, was that the entire action was commanded, not by the United States or any other military, but by the Blackwater contractors in the building. The proof is the video one of them took and posted on the web.

The other event, which occurred a few days before, at the city of Falluja, was grimmer still. In March 2004, the US military were involved in a massacre at a school in the city on Hay Nazzal street. Following the massacre, the US military moved out but had encircled the city, and there had been running battles all over Falluja in the days leading up to the end of March. In circumstances that remain unclear, four poorly armed Blackwater contractors drove into the city in a Pajero jeep. They had not explained what they were doing to the US military with whom they had spent the night. They had not explained what mission they were on. They had not long entered the city before they were ambushed and all four were killed. But it didn't end there. Here is how Scahill describes the next sighting that anyone had of the four dead contractors:

> 'The charred remains of the Blackwater contractors were still hanging from the Falluja bridge when news of the ambush began to spread across the globe. "They cant do that to Americans," said Captain Douglas Zembiac, as he watched the scene on TV in a mess hall at a military base outside Falluja.'

But it wasn't the perpetrators of the murders who would pay for what had happened to 'Americans'. No one knew who the killers were. In the months and years that followed, the American military twice attacked Falluja, making no pretence that this was legitimate war. It was revenge for what had happened to the Blackwater contractors. About 90 per cent of the population of the city was displaced by the two American attacks. An unknown number of Iraqis, certainly not less than 2,000 to 4,000 men, women and many children, were killed as American bullets went through walls that were never intended to stop gunfire, and didn't. The two attacks on Falluja were classic mass punishments and were aggressive war against mainly unarmed, and unprotected civilians. They were war crimes at every level; in their motivation and their execution.

So who or what are Blackwater?

Blackwater is a private military corporation, initially set up to cash in on the process of privatisation of the military that was launched by the disgraced US former defence secretary Donald Rumsfeld on 10 September 2001. That day Rumsfeld described the Pentagon, in terms of its inept and centralised planning of the US military, as '... an adversary that poses a threat, a serious threat, to the security of the United States of America'.

According to Scahill, Rumsfeld called for a wholesale shift in the running of the Pentagon, supplanting the old Department of Defense bureaucracy with a new model, one based on the private sector. What Rumsfeld got was Blackwater. But what he got before that, in fact the day after his speech, was an Al Qaeda hijacked civil airliner slamming into the west wall of the Pentagon. Rumsfeld's mistaken idea of who the enemy actually was did not alter his determination to build civilian contractors into the US military.

In a cabinet almost entirely recruited from arms companies there was no opposition to bringing mercenaries into every area of military life, short of employing them directly in front line combat duties. Standing ready to accept the largess that paid for this policy was Erik Prince, a right wing religious neocon from Holland, in Michigan. He had set up Blackwater after he left the US Navy SEALS in 1998, in the Great Dismal Swamp area of North Carolina. It was meant to be a training and target shooting facility for training Navy SEALS and law enforcement agencies. But even as the initial 4,000 acres was being brought into use, Prince, a multimillionaire, was running a sophisticated and heavily funded lobbying operation in Washington. It is hard to say to what extent Rumsfeld's policy of privatisation was influenced by the Prince lobby but, taken together with the Al Qaeda attack, it paid dividends for Prince. When the US attacked Iraq in March 2003, the attacking forces were accompanied by up to 100,000 civilian contractors, of whom the most heavily armed and highest paid were Prince's Blackwater mercenaries. The formal job of the Blackwater staff was to provide security for the occupation administration. Blackwater has lost 30 or 40 employees in Iraq. What has not been counted are the civilians killed by Blackwater, in the many encounters described by Scahill.

This is an immensely worthwhile and carefully compiled book. It is a tribute to the journalism for which America was once famous. It describes in great detail the links between the politicians in the Bush administration and the neocons and right wing religious fanatics in the business community, each feeding off the other and determined to change, by force of arms, the infrastructure of the Middle East. But Scahill also demonstrates clearly that, without the unfettered access this crowd got to US taxpayers' dollars, neither they nor their wars could exist. In the end it is an indictment of the failure of the American Congress and Senate to hold the administration to the truths of the constitution and, perhaps more important, to prevent the squandering of US treasure.

Take the arms companies out of government

Every year, around £900 million of public money is spent subsidising the sale of UK weaponry around the world.

Why? Because arms companies wield immense political power and influence within government.

It's time to stop arms companies calling the shots.

For a free Call the Shots campaign pack, please call 020 7281 0297 or email enquiries@caat.org.uk

www.caat.org.uk

Star Wars

David Webb

David Webb is Professor of Engineering Modelling and co-director of the Praxis Centre for the Study of Information and Technology in Peace, Conflict Resolution and Human Rights at Leeds Metropolitan University. In June 2007, he addressed the Security and Defence Sub-Committee of the European Parliament on plans for anti-ballistic missile systems in Europe. This is what he said.

Does Europe need an anti-missile defence shield? The question is being posed at this time because of the recent request by the United States to position bases in the Czech Republic and Poland as part of its own National Missile Defence (NMD) system.

To help tackle this question I would like to consider four associated ones:
- What is the threat of missile attack?
- How effective is missile defence likely to be?
- What are the consequences of deploying a European missile defence system?
- Are there alternative forms of action?

What is Missile Defence?

The US Ground Based Mid Course Defence (GMD) system currently consists of some 15 silo-based interceptors at Fort Greely, Alaska and two at Vandenberg Air Force Base, California. There are also associated ground-based early warning and tracking radars, including those at Thule in Greenland and Fylingdales in North Yorkshire in England (recently upgraded for its role in National Missile Defence), and a $1 billion sea-based X-band radar to track, discriminate and assess targets from a mobile, semi-submersible platform in the Aleutian Islands between the Alaska and Kamchatka peninsulas.

The United States proposes that 10 more interceptors be based in Poland, and a modified X-band radar system moved to the Czech Republic. The US claims it needs to have these sites operational by 2012 in order to counter any possible future threat from Iran or North Korea.

Although originally conceived as a system for long range missiles aimed at the United States, the suggestion now is that it be combined with the missile defence system under consideration by Nato to form an integrated European defence system. A Charter for an Active Layered Theatre Ballistic Missile Defence (ALTBMD) was approved by Nato in March 2005. The 20-year cost of this undertaking is reported to be 1 billion euros and, in addition, some 20 billion euros would be spent by individual member states on missile defence batteries. Increasing costs cause some concern; most. European Nato states are unable or unwilling to increase spending on defence as other concerns such as education and health take precedence. Despite this, Nato is considering extending the system to protect population centres – leading to possible eventual integration with the US National Missile Defence system.

What is the threat?

None of the European Union member states appears to have any immediate concern about the threat of a missile attack. There are differences of opinion within Nato on the assessment of threats from 'states of concern', but even Nato's own parliamentary assembly does not have immediate access to classified threat assessments carried out on its behalf. It does seem odd that parliamentary democracies are expected to act on and pay for threat assessments and feasibility studies that they are not even allowed to see.

The United States is very concerned about the threat of missile attack. Successive US governments have continued to fund and develop a cut-down version of President Reagan's unrealistic idea of a missile defence umbrella. In justification of their 2008 budget request for European National Missile Defence sites, the US Missile Defence Agency stated that the bases are needed to improve protection of the United States by protecting its existing European based radars, and providing additional and earlier intercept opportunities. In addition, they would extend this protection to allies and friends and demonstrate an international support for ballistic missile defence. The major threat to these installations and/or the United States itself is believed to come from Iran. Let's examine this threat in more detail.

Currently, Iran has no nuclear warheads, and may not obtain any for some time (if at all). It does, however, possess a medium-range ballistic missile with a range of 1,200kms, but has denied that it is developing the next generation with a range of 2,900kms. Although that denial may be controversial, what is certain is that they are not developing the Shahab-5 which, with a range of 6,000kms, would be able to reach greater parts of Europe but still not threaten the United States (some 10,000kms away). It has been predicted that Iran may possibly develop missiles that could reach the United States by 2015 at the earliest. However, placing a primitive nuclear warhead on an unreliable ballistic missile would be a risky and costly business. Even if successful, it could result in a retaliation so devastating that it would mean national suicide.

The United States is preparing for a future potential threat rather than an imminent one. Their desire to place interceptors in Europe requires European co-operation and this can be hastened by persuading Europe that there is an imminent threat to them. There is no evidence that Iran wishes to attack Europe. Their reason for developing a nuclear capability (if they are) could well be the same as that claimed by all nuclear states – for deterrence purposes.

Effectiveness

In 2002, President George W. Bush unilaterally withdrew the United States from the 1972 Anti-Ballistic Missile (ABM) Treaty in order to build an 'effective' missile defence system. Five years later, the system has still to prove that it can work in realistic circumstances (see box). During controlled tests, under unrealistic conditions where information is made available in advance that would not be supplied by an enemy, successful intercept has been achieved in only six out of 11 attempts. The satellite networks required for detecting missile launches and tracking trajectories are years behind schedule and way over budget, and an effective and operational command and control network has not been established. The annual report of the Pentagon's testing office, released earlier this year, stated that a lack of flight-test data 'limits confidence in assessments' of the system.

A report by the US Government Accountability Office (GAO), in March 2007, concluded that the system 'has not completed sufficient flight testing to provide a high level of confidence that [it] can reliably intercept inter-continental ballistic missiles'. In addition, the system can readily be overcome by numbers. Ten interceptors would be seriously challenged by eleven or more real or decoy warheads.

There is an added complication for the proposed European interceptor site. The ground-based interceptor missiles in Poland will need only two-stage missiles rather than the three-stage interceptors in Alaska and California. Research and development on a two-stage interceptor has only just begun. Given the problems encountered when developing the existing interceptor missile, can we expect a much easier time for the development of the new one?

There is also a question as to whether testing the new intercepts would be illegal under the Intermediate-Range Nuclear Forces Treaty, which eliminated nuclear and conventional ground-launched ballistic and cruise missiles with ranges of 500 to 5,500kms. If it can't be tested, how will we know if it works?

So, with missile defence we seem to be considering the use of interceptor missiles that have not so far been developed, as part of a costly, unproven system that is easily overcome, to defend against a threat that probably doesn't exist.

What are the consequences?

The cost of building the bases in Poland and the Czech Republic is estimated to be some $3.5 billion. There is also a probability that the programme would later be extended to cover all European territory by the inclusion of sea-based missiles and missile tracking systems in space at considerable (but unspecified) extra cost. The technological problems encountered in developments of this kind are complex and cannot be accurately predicted. Massive extra costs and overruns are common.

Perhaps the biggest problem with missile defence, however, is how its development is perceived by others. It is argued by some that a workable missile shield would enable the United States to strike first with nuclear weapons as any limited retaliation could be dealt with effectively. Even if this is not the intention, it is easy to see how the antagonistic nature of US defence policy leads many states to this conclusion. The highly accurate nuclear missiles in the US arsenal are not required by deterrence, but could be used to destroy enemy missile silos. The proposed new US National Missile Defence bases are in states formerly in an alliance with Russia, which the US Secretary of Defense Robert Gates recently included in a list of potential threats to US security. Is it so surprising, then, that Russia has reacted strongly to the National Missile Defence proposals, calling them an 'unfriendly step', with President Putin threatening to target European sites with nuclear weapons?

The United States says that the missiles are not aimed at Russia. However, an analysis of the geographic locations and missile trajectories shows that the radar and interceptors could be deployed against Russian missiles from some of its western launch sites and even though 10 interceptors clearly do not pose a threat to the 500 or so missiles in Russia's nuclear arsenal, a Russian Foreign Ministry statement suggests that 'one cannot ignore the fact that US offensive weapons, combined with the missile defence being created, can turn into a strategic complex capable of delivering an incapacitating blow'.

Missile Defence Doesn't Work

Theodore Postol is Professor of Science, Technology and National Security Policy at the Massachusetts Institute of Technology. He is a former scientific and policy adviser to the Pentagon on nuclear weapons and related matters, including missile defense. On 3 July 2007, following President Putin's meeting with President Bush in Maine, he participated in a discussion on Democracy Now radio chaired by Amy Goodman, from which these excerpts are taken. The full discussion is available online (www.democracynow.org).

'... The missile defense that the Bush administration has proposed is going to have a radar in the Czech Republic and missile interceptors in northern Poland. Now, the administration has stated that this system could not engage Russian intercontinental ballistic missiles if they were fired toward the United States, and that does not appear to be true, if one accepts the capabilities of the system as described by the Missile Defense Agency. We've done an analysis that shows that this is not a true statement. And in fact, we've also looked a little bit at variants of the Putin proposal, and we find that placing radars much closer to the launch sites, that is to say to the postulated Iranian missile threat in Azerbaijan or in Turkey, would in fact do a much better job of actually achieving the defensive capability that the Bush administration states it wants to achieve ...

The problem that adds even more complexity to this issue is the completely unrealistic character of the technical system that the administration claims will do missile defence. In fact, my earlier statement was caveated in a very important way. I said 'if' the system components work as the Missile Defence Agency claims they would. In fact, these missile defence components will never work the way the Missile Defence Agency claims they would. But, in fact, the United States claims they would work, and the Russians, at some level, have taken us at our word. So we've got the worst of both worlds. We've got a system that the Russians treat or perceive or treat politically as if it has some capability, which means this raises big political questions ..., and at the same time we have a system that really will provide no realistic defensive capability ...

The United States proposal to include Russia in further cooperation on missile defences has generated an interesting response from President Putin who has suggested joint US-Russian use of an early warning radar in Gabala, Azerbaijan. This radar would give good coverage of missiles from Iran but not of Russian launches, because of an intervening range of mountains. However, the United States has now said this cannot replace the proposed Czech radar.

Within Europe there is some unease about the deteriorating US-Russian relationship. German Foreign Minister Frank-Walter Steinmeier has been quoted in a newspaper article in March as saying that, in protecting against a possible Iranian threat, 'the price of security must not be new suspicion or, worse still, fresh insecurity'. He also stated that, '[W]e cannot allow a missile defense system to be either a reason or a pretext for a new arms race'.

> The MIT Lincoln Laboratory ... was involved in concealing the failure of a very critical missile defence experiment, which was supposed to show whether or not the current system could tell the difference between a basketball-sized balloon and warheads, and the system was unable to do this. So this basically means that in no realistic combat situation that is imaginable, the system has no chance of working. The MIT Corporation, including its board of directors, known as the Executive Committee, have been involved, in my opinion – in my opinion, have been involved in concealing this from the Congress and the American people. And I've been pursuing this matter, and I think the Congress will almost certainly be picking up on this ...
>
> ... What my colleagues and I found is that the Patriot was essentially a total failure in the Gulf War of 1991. This is now widely accepted as truth. When we first raised the question, the US Army had told the Congress that the Patriot was 96% effective in the Gulf War of 1991. We found that it almost certainly failed to intercept a single Scud warhead in the entire war. So this was an important result, not so much because of its implications for the war of 1991, since very little was done in terms of military consequence from the incoming Scuds, but it was very important in the political debate that followed, where people were trying to make this falsely represented success into an argument for a complete and comprehensive missile defense that would be global ...
>
> What Putin proposed – and I think it's a fluid proposal – he proposed to make a large early warning radar, that is currently operating in Azerbaijan and looks out over Iran, available to the United States for monitoring Iranian missile tests. Now, this radar is not an ideal radar for monitoring missile defence tests, but it actually would do a pretty good job in assisting a missile defence of the kind that the United States has proposed for Europe in acquiring attacking warheads so that they could be engaged. I'm not arguing this is a good idea. I'm just simply explaining that this radar could play a very useful practical role. So I was in Washington, and all of the people are repeating these arguments that sound plausible but have no basis, that somehow this radar is inappropriate. It's a fine radar for that purpose.'

The arms race may already be with us. Russia has announced new additions to its armoury to overcome the missile shield, and missile defence encourages nuclear states to enlarge their arsenals so as to keep their deterrent effective. It can therefore be accused of being responsible for contravening the Non-Proliferation Treaty.

Ballistic Missile Defence is not mentioned in the European Security and Defence Policy (ESDP), or European Union Strategies on Security or Weapons of Mass Destruction. The Secretary General of the Council of the European Union, Javier Solana, has said that the EU has no plans to participate in a US anti-missile system but that its member states are free to join if they wish. However, members may consider that the relevance of the issue to the whole of Europe would suggest that Poland and the Czech Republic should at least consult with other member states before making a deal with the United States.

So how will this situation develop? Will European Union member states continue to develop their own missile defence systems individually within the framework of the Nato/US proposals? If so, then it appears that the European Union has accepted by default that Iran is a threat to European security. This surely is too important an issue to be decided in such a way? It will have major consequences in terms of European security and Middle East policies. There needs to be a much more serious and prolonged debate.

We should also not forget the problems associated with hosting US bases. The UK experience can inform the Czech and Polish governments that they are very unlikely to have control over launching procedure decisions. The 500 or so US staff to be employed will not be subject to Polish or Czech law. It is clear that the majority of the citizens (more than 60 per cent) of these two countries, especially those that live near the proposed sites, do not want the bases.

From a future international perspective, any European systems integrated into US missile defence could eventually be used to target space-based interceptors which the Pentagon is keen to develop. Do we in Europe really want to be involved in the weaponisation of space? In 2005, Canada withdrew cooperation with US missile defence because its citizens considered it a first step to the weaponisation of space.

The Alternatives

Participants at an International Conference against the Militarization of Europe, which was held in Prague on 5 May, put their names to a declaration which included the words:

> 'The governments of Poland and the Czech Republic ... risk ... jeopardising the present framework of international agreements on nuclear non-proliferation and conventional arms control throughout the world, but especially in Europe. What we really need is disarmament as a precondition to peace and genuine human security. To face the impending ecological crisis we need international cooperation and trust, not confrontation.'

The people of Europe have high expectations of their governments. Extending missile defence to European Nato allies may seem logical to some, but it will mean that diplomacy and multilateral arms control are sacrificed to the unilateral use of force – as was the case in Iraq. Clearly, the developing US agenda of missile defence does not fit with the cooperative security model that European governments support. There are other ways.

The statement to the Preparatory Committee for the 2010 Nuclear Non-Proliferation Treaty Review Conference by the European Union's Ambassador includes the following:

> 'The European Union attaches a clear priority to the negotiations without precondition in the Conference on Disarmament, of a treaty banning the production of fissile material for nuclear weapons or other explosive devices, as a means to strengthen disarmament and non-proliferation. It constitutes a priority that waits to be seized.'

European Union countries must seize it and encourage others to do the same. If we are really concerned about nuclear weapons proliferation we must pursue with increased vigour a Fissile Material Cut-Off Treaty, develop new international monitoring systems, and abide by and strengthen the Nuclear Non-Proliferation Treaty. If we are worried about ballistic missiles we can negotiate a new Anti-Ballistic Missile Treaty or a missile test ban, and work for missile-free zones. If we are troubled about the weaponisation of space we can work harder for more cooperative agreements for the use of space, a new Outer Space Treaty, and a ban on space weapons. We could make a real attempt to rid the world once and for all from the threat of nuclear annihilation by seriously pursuing a Nuclear Weapons Convention.

But agreements must be effective. The Hague Code of Conduct against Ballistic Missile Proliferation, agreed in November 2002, established both international norms against proliferation and modest confidence building measures, and has attracted a great deal of diplomatic support. However, much more effort is needed to turn it into a set of legally binding obligations and to provide real inducements to states such as North Korea and Iran to abandon missile development. Without these, the Code will have little effect.

In the 2003 European Union document entitled 'A Secure Europe in a Better World, European Security Strategy', we find the following:

> 'In contrast to the massive visible threat in the Cold War, none of the new threats is purely military; nor can any be tackled by purely military means. Each requires a mixture of instruments.'

Missile Defence is an example of an instrument applied too late. There is a danger that if a convincing defence against missiles did exist, we would put too much faith in that and not enough effort in preventing situations getting to the stage where it might be deployed.

The world is looking to the European Union for inspiration – the threat of war between traditional enemies in Europe has been eradicated in a generation. This is a tremendous accomplishment. By building a wall around Europe we would be resorting to the politics of the past. We should be proud of our achievements and engage with states outside the European Union to build mutual trust and security. Indeed, if we are to survive as a civilization, as a species, even as a planet, we need to learn how to develop technologies for a positive future and tolerate cultural differences. This is our greatest challenge and to fail is unthinkable.

Common Sense and Nuclear Warfare
by Bertrand Russell

Available for the first time in many years, *Common Sense and Nuclear Warfare* presents Russell's keen insights into the threat of nuclear conflict, and his argument that the only way to end this threat is to end war itself.

Written at the height of the Cold War, this volume is crucial for understanding Russell's involvement in the Campaign for Nuclear Disarmament and his passionate campaigning for peace.

It remains an extremely important book in today's uncertain nuclear world, and is essential reading for all those interested in Russell and postwar history.

Includes a new introduction by Ken Coates, Chairman of The Bertrand Russell Peace Foundation

Paperback Price: £11.99 | ISBN: 9780415249959
Hardback Price: £55.00 | ISBN: 9780415259942

www.routledge.com   Available from all good bookshops

Nuclear disarmament for Scotland

Alex Salmond MSP

Alex Salmond is First Minister of Scotland. On 15 October 2007, he wrote to the Ambassadors of the 122 countries that have signed the Nuclear Non-Proliferation Treaty.

Your Excellency,

I am writing to you, as representative of a State Party to the Nuclear Non-Proliferation Treaty (NPT), to inform you of the Scottish Government's views and determination to play as constructive a part as possible in pursuing our country's nuclear disarmament obligations under the NPT. We also intend to explore the possibility of taking up observer status at future NPT meetings, so that we can more directly and effectively represent the aspirations and interests of Scotland's people. In the event that we do seek that status, I would hope we would be able to count on your government's support.

As you may know, the United Kingdom currently deploys a 4-submarine Trident nuclear weapon system from the Faslane Naval Base in Scotland. The UK also stores up to 200 nuclear warheads a few miles further along the coast, in Coulport. Last March the UK government pushed through the Westminster Parliament a preliminary decision to renew the Trident system, thereby signalling its intention to continue to make and deploy nuclear weapons beyond 2050. The majority of Scottish people and their elected representatives oppose these deployments.

In May, for the first time since the nuclear age began in 1945, the people of Scotland elected a government that is opposed to nuclear weapons. On 14 June, the Scottish Parliament debated the following motion in relation to the UK Government's policy on nuclear weapons:

> 'That the Parliament congratulates the majority of Scottish MPs for voting on 14 March 2007 to reject the replacement of Trident, recognises that decisions on matters of defence are matters within the responsibility of the UK Government and Parliament and calls on the UK Government not to go ahead at this time with the proposal in the White Paper, *The Future of the United Kingdom's Nuclear Deterrent.*'

The Scottish Parliament showed clear and overwhelming opposition to the UK

Government's plan to replace its Trident nuclear weapons system (by 71 votes to 16, with 39 abstentions), and widespread support for this Government's vision of a Scotland without nuclear weapons.

During the debate, the Scottish Government signalled its intention to reflect on the views of the majority of Scots and carefully consider which aspects of the UK Government's plans to replace Trident impact on our responsibilities in Scotland under devolution. We made it clear that we will do all that we can, in light of those responsibilities, to persuade the UK Government to change its stance both on the replacement programme and on the general principle of maintaining and deploying nuclear weapons.

Recognising that there are a range of views on the constitutional future of Scotland, we have embarked on a National Conversation with the Scottish public on the options for constitutional change leading to further development of the way we govern ourselves. As part of this debate on Scotland's constitutional future, we will be holding a high level meeting of key stakeholders from across Scottish life to discuss the implications of the replacement of Trident and what a Scotland without nuclear weapons might look like.

I would like to assure you of Scotland's deep commitment to international peace and security, and our desire to participate in making the case for implementation of the nuclear disarmament and non-proliferation provisions of the NPT and other relevant international agreements and treaties. Please do not hesitate to contact me if you or your government wish to discuss these issues further.

Scotland's future without nuclear weapons

Rob Edwards

Alex Salmond has made a major bid to win international backing for his government's campaign to rid Scotland of nuclear weapons. Scotland's First Minister has written to 122 countries highlighting the nation's opposition to the deployment of Trident nuclear warheads on the Clyde, and his determination to try and block the United Kingdom government's decision to replace Trident.

Salmond is also asking the countries to support a request for Scotland to be given observer status at future meetings of the parties to the Nuclear Non-Proliferation Treaty (NPT), an international agreement to limit the spread of nuclear weapons.

The first minister's move, on the eve of the Scottish government's Trident summit in Glasgow, has been hailed as a potential breakthrough by disarmament experts. The summit will hear evidence from a Scottish advocate, John Mayer, that nuclear weapons are illegal under international law and the Scottish parliament would be 'well within its competence' to pass legislation preventing crimes committed by weapons of mass destruction. 'The law of the whole world is against Trident. The Scottish parliament stands at a turning point to outlaw its threat or use, and in doing so will lead the world into a safer 21st century,' said Mayer.

Salmond's letter is addressed to the UK ambassadors of 122 countries party to the Non-Proliferation Treaty. 'In May, for the first time since the nuclear age began in 1945, the people of Scotland elected a government that is opposed to nuclear weapons,' he declared. The Scottish government was planning to do 'all that we can' to persuade UK ministers to change their mind on Trident, said Salmond. 'The majority of Scottish people and their elected representatives oppose these deployments.'

A decision to replace Trident was taken by former Prime Minister, Tony Blair, and pushed through the Commons in March, despite a

Rob Edwards is Environment Editor of the Sunday Herald *in Scotland, which published this article on 21 October 2007.*

Labour revolt. But a majority of Scottish Members of Parliament opposed the decision, as have an overwhelming majority of Members of the Scottish Parliament.

The Trident summit will be opened by the Deputy First Minister, Nicola Sturgeon, and closed by the Scottish Minister for Parliamentary Business, Bruce Crawford. 'There are few more important issues in the world today than nuclear weapons proliferation,' Crawford said. 'As a country we have every right to give voice to our opposition to nuclear weapons on Scottish soil.'

Green Member of the Scottish Parliament Patrick Harvie, who will speak at the summit, said: 'We all have an obligation to do what we can to stop the Westminster government forcing another generation of nuclear weapons onto Scotland.'

New research released by the Scottish Government suggests that opposition to nuclear weapons was a significant factor in causing voters to switch from Labour to the Scottish National Party (SNP) at the May election. There was 'a compelling case Trident was at least part of the reason for Labour losing support in 2007', said the author of the research, Robert Johns from the University of Strathclyde. A YouGov poll in May showed 58% of people in Scotland opposed Trident, up four to six points on previous surveys.

Reprinted with grateful acknowledgements

THE BERTRAND RUSSELL PEACE FOUNDATION
DOSSIER

RUSSELL TRIBUNAL ON PALESTINE

The organizers of the Tribunal have issued this appeal for support, which has already met with a positive response. The Tribunal was initiated by Pierre Galand in Brussels and Robert Kissous in Paris.

The Russell Tribunal on Palestine will work rigorously and in the same spirit as the Tribunal on Vietnam that sat in 1967, under the presidency of Jean-Paul Sartre. The Tribunal will have to judge breaches of international law, of which the Palestinians are victims, and which deprive the Palestinian people of a sovereign State.

The Advisory Opinion that was given by the International Court of Justice at The Hague on 9 July 2004 sums up those violations and concludes, in particular, with the obligation for Israel to dismantle the Wall and to compensate the Palestinians for all the damage suffered from this construction. This Opinion recalls, at §163D, that

> 'All States are under an obligation not to recognize the illegal situation resulting from the construction of the wall, and not to render aid or assistance in maintaining the situation created by such construction; all State parties to the Fourth Geneva Convention relative to the Protection of Civilians Persons in Time of War of 12 August 1949 have, in addition, the obligation, while respecting the United Nations Charter and international law, to ensure compliance by Israel with international law as embodied in that Convention.'

This Opinion was confirmed on 24 July 2004 by resolution ES-10/15 of the General Assembly of the United Nations, which was adopted by 150 States Members. The General Assembly 'demands that Israel, the occupying Power, comply with its legal obligations as mentioned in the advisory opinion' and 'calls upon all States Members of the United Nations to comply with their legal obligations as mentioned in the advisory opinion'.

Drawing in particular on the Advisory Opinion and the UN resolution, the Russell Tribunal on Palestine will reaffirm the primacy/supremacy of international law as the basis for the settlement of the Israeli-Palestinian conflict. It will identify breaches to the application of the law and will condemn all the perpetrators before international public opinion.

Your support to this Tribunal will give it the moral weight necessary to advance the cause of justice and law in this part of the world.

Ken Coates
Chairman of the Bertrand Russell Peace Foundation
Nurit Peled
Sakharov Prize 2001
Leila Shahid
General Delegate of Palestine to the European Union,
Belgium, Luxembourg

An initial list of members of the Support Committee of the Russell Tribunal includes:

Andreas Van Agt – Prime Minister of the Netherlands from 1977 to 1982
Henri Alleg – Journalist – France
Martin Almada – Lawyer, Writer, Right Livelihood Award 2002 – Paraguay
Kader Asmal – Professor, Former Minister, MP – South Africa
Raymond and Lucie Aubrac – Former Members of the French Resistance
Etienne Balibar – Professor Emeritus – France
Russell Banks – Writer, President of the International Parliament of Writers – USA
Mohammed Bedjaoui – Former President of the International Court of Justice (The Hague), Former Minister of Foreign Affairs of Algeria
Ahmed Ben Bella – First President of the Republic of Algeria
Amar Bentoumi – President Emeritus of the International Association of Democratic Lawyers – Algeria
John Berger – Writer – UK
Howard Brenton – Writer – UK
Carmel Budiardjo – Right Livelihood Award 1995 – UK
Judith Butler – Professor of Rhetoric and Comparative Literature – USA
Monique Chemillier-Gendreau – Professor Emeritus – France
Noam Chomsky – Professor, Massachusetts Institute of Technology – USA
Vicenzo Consolo – Writer – Italy
Mairead Corrigan Maguire – Nobel Peace Prize 1976 – UK
Miguel Angel Estrella – Pianist, Former Argentinean Ambassador to UNESCO
Irene Fernandez – Right Livelihood Award 2005 – Malaysia
Cees Flinterman – Director of the Netherlands Institute of Human Rights
Eduardo Galeano – Writer – Uruguay
Johan Galtung – Founder of Transcend, Right Livelihood Award 1987 – Norway
Geraud de Geouffre de la Pradelle – Professor Emeritus – France
Juan Goytisolo – Writer – Spain
Trevor Griffiths – Writer – UK
Gisele Halimi – Lawyer, Former French Ambassador to UNESCO
Jeff Halper – Coordinator of Israeli Committee against House Demolitions

Mohammed Harbi – Historian – France/Algeria
Eric Hazan – Writer – France
Stephane Hessel – Ambassador of France
François Houtart – Professor Emeritus – Belgium
Albert Jacquard – University Professor – France
Alain Joxe – Director of Studies at the School of Advanced Studies in Social Sciences – France
Milan Kucan – Former President of the Republic of Slovenia
Felicia Langer – Lawyer, Writer, Right Livelihood Award 1990 – Germany
Paul Laverty – Writer – UK
Ken Loach – Filmmaker – UK
François Maspero – Writer – France
Gustave Massiah – Chairman, Centre of Research for Development – France
Avi Mograbi – Filmmaker – Israel
Radhia Nasraoui – Human Rights Lawyer – Tunisia
Simone Paris de Bollardière – Movement for Non-violence Alternative – France
Tamar Pelleg-Sryck – Human Rights Lawyer – Israel
Harold Pinter – Writer, Nobel Prize for Literature 2005 – UK
François Rigaux – Professor Emeritus – Belgium
François Roux – Lawyer – France
Elias Sanbar – Writer – Palestine
José Saramago – Nobel Prize for Literature 1998 – Portugal
Vandana Shiva – Director of the Research Foundation for Science, Technology and Ecology, Right Livelihood Award 1993 – India
Sulak Sivaraksa – Professor, Right Livelihood Award 1995 – Thailand
Philippe Texier – Magistrate and Member of the UN Human Rights Committee – France
Gerard Toulouse – Physician – France
Brian Urquhart – Former Undersecretary-General of the United Nations – UK
Michel Warschawski – Activist – Israel
Francisco Whitaker – Right Livelihood Award 2006 – Brazil
Betty Williams – Nobel Peace Prize 1976 – UK
Jody Williams – Nobel Peace Prize 1997 – USA

PALESTINE: UN SHOULD LEAVE QUARTET

The UN human rights envoy for the Palestinian territories, Professor John Dugard, was interviewed by Jon Snow on Channel 4 News on 15 July 2007.

Snow: Professor Dugard, surely in a sense you are calling for the UN to disengage from the Quartet just at the moment when the Americans have finally said its time for a Palestinian State?

Dugard: My complaint about the Quartet is that for years it has ignored the human rights aspect of the dispute. I am delighted that there is now serious talk of a conference which it is hoped will bring about the real solution to the question, but I do think that in this conference full attention should be given to human rights issues.

For instance, there are issues such as the wall that Israel is building in the Palestinian territory. They've increased the number of settlements. They've increased the number of checkpoints. There is the whole question of military incursions and arrests of Palestinians.

Snow: It's an interesting thing that you should raise that because quoted in the British newspapers over this last weekend Tony Blair, the envoy for the Quartet, has expressed shock and surprise at some of the damage that has been done to the Palestinian territories by the wall. Do you think that perhaps the West is, at last, waking up to what is going on there?

Dugard: I'm surprised that Mr Blair was not aware of this when he was Prime Minister because I'm quite sure that his Foreign Office was informing him about what had happened. After all there was a 2004 decision, advisory opinion, of the International Court of Justice holding that the construction of the wall is illegal and Mr Blair distanced himself from that finding.

Snow: Can I just ask you then, how would the UN's hand be strengthened if it was disengaged from the Quartet?

Dugard: My complaint is that the United Nations is no longer seen as an impartial and evenhanded mediator in the dispute between Palestinians and Israelis. I believe its absolutely essential that the United Nations should be seen to be objective and impartial but, by siding too much with Israel and by failing to take account of the violation of Palestinian human rights, the United Nations has lost that image of impartiality. There is no doubt that the United Nations is being used to legitimise the Quartet and if that is its sole purpose I believe the United Nations should reconsider its position.

BUSH & AZNAR TALK WAR

On 22 February 2003, a few weeks before the invasion if Iraq, President Bush spoke with then Prime Minister Aznar of Spain, at his ranch in Crawford, Texas. Condoleezza Rice, National Security Advisor, was also present. A transcript of their conversation was published in El Pais, *the Spanish newspaper, in September 2007. It gives a sharp insight into the President's preparations for war. This translation was prepared by Juan Cole (www.juancole.com), to whom we are grateful for permission to use it.*

President Bush: We are in favour of getting a second resolution in the Security Council and would want to do it quickly. We would want to announce it Monday or Tuesday [24 or 25 February 2003].

Prime Minister Aznar: Better Tuesday, after the meeting of the Council of General Affairs of the European Union. It is important to maintain the momentum gained by the resolution at the summit of the European Union [which had taken place in Brussels on Monday 17 February]. We would prefer to wait until Tuesday.

Bush: It could be in the evening Monday, considering the time difference. In any case, the next week. We will see that the resolution is written so that it does not contain obligatory steps [for Iraq], that it does not mention the use of force, and that it states that Saddam Hussein has been unable to fulfil his obligations. That type of resolution can be voted for by many people. It would be something similar to the one passed regarding Kosovo [10 June 1999].

Aznar: Would it be presented to the Security Council before, and independently of, a parallel declaration?

Condoleezza Rice: In fact there would not be a parallel declaration. We are thinking about as simple a resolution as possible, without many details regarding [Iraq's] obligations — such that Saddam Hussein could use them as stages and consequently could neglect to fulfil them. We are speaking with Blix [head of the inspectors of the United Nations] and others of his team to get ideas that can serve to introduce the resolution.

Bush: Saddam Hussein will not change and will continue playing games. The moment has come to be rid of him. That's the way it is. As for me, from now on I will try to tone down the rhetoric as much as possible, while we seek approval of the resolution. If somebody uses a veto, we will go. [Russia, China and France have, along with the United States and the United Kingdom, the right to a veto in the Security Council by virtue of being permanent members.]

Saddam Hussein is not disarming. We have to take him right now. We have shown an incredible degree of patience so far. There are two weeks left. In two weeks we will be militarily ready. I believe that we will get the second resolution. In the Security Council we have the three African members [Cameroon, Angola and Guinea], the Chileans, and the Mexicans. I will speak with all of them, also with Putin, naturally. We will be in Baghdad at the end of March. There is a 15 per cent possibility that Saddam Hussein will die or flee. But that possibility will not exist until we have demonstrated our resolve. The Egyptians are talking to Saddam Hussein. It seems that he has indicated that he is willing to go into exile if he can take a billion dollars with him and all the information that he wants on weapons of mass destruction. [Muammar] Gaddafi told Berlusconi that Saddam Hussein wants to go away. Mubarak tells us that in these circumstances it is entirely possible that he will be assassinated.

We would like to act with the mandate of the United Nations. If we act militarily we will do it with great precision, tightly focusing on our objectives. We will decimate the troops loyal to him, and the regular army quickly will recognize what is going on. We have sent a very clear message to Saddam's generals: we will treat them like war criminals. We know that they have accumulated an enormous amount of dynamite to demolish bridges and other infrastructure and to blow up the oil wells. We foresee occupying those wells very quickly. Also, the Saudis will help us by putting on the market all the petroleum that is necessary. We are developing a package of very extensive humanitarian aid. We can win without destruction. We are already planning for a post-Saddam Iraq, and I believe that there are good bases for a better future. Iraq has a relatively good bureaucracy and a civil society. It can be organized as a federal system. Meanwhile, we are doing everything possible to take care of the political needs of our friends and allies.

Aznar: It is very important to have a resolution. It is not the same to act with it as without it. It would be very advisable to have a majority in the Security Council that supported that resolution. In fact, it is important to have it passed by a majority, even if someone exercises a veto. Let us consider that the text of the resolution would have, among other things, to state that Saddam Hussein has lost his opportunity.

Bush: Yes, by all means. It would be better to have a reference to 'necessary means' [a reference to the type of UN resolution that authorizes the use of 'all necessary means'].

Aznar: Saddam Hussein has not co-operated, has not been disarmed; we would have to summarize his breaches and to send a more detailed message. That would allow, for example, Mexico to move [a reference to a change in its negative position on the second resolution, the extent of which Aznar could have known about from the lips of President Vicente Fox on Friday 21 February, in Mexico City].

Bush: The resolution will be custom-made in such a way that it will help you. I don't care much about the content.

Aznar: We will send you some sample texts.

Bush: We do not have any text. Only a criterion: that Saddam Hussein disarm. We cannot allow Saddam Hussein to drag things out until the summer. After all, this last stage has already lasted four months, and this is more than enough time to disarm.

Aznar: Having a text would allow us to sponsor it and to be its co-authors, and to arrange for many others to sponsor it.

Bush: Perfect.

Aznar: Next Wednesday [26 February] I will meet with Chirac. The resolution will already have begun to circulate.

Bush: It seems to me all very good. Chirac knows the reality perfectly. Their intelligence services have explained it to him. The Arabs are transmitting a very clear message to Chirac: Saddam Hussein must go. The problem is that Chirac thinks he is Mister Arab, but in fact he is making their lives impossible. But I do not want to have any rivalry with Chirac. We have different points of view, but I would like that to be all. Give him my best regards. Really! The less rivalry he feels exists between us, the better it will be for everyone.

Aznar: How to combine the resolution with the report of the inspectors?

Condoleezza Rice: Actually there will not be a report on 28 February, but the inspectors will present a report written on 1 March. We don't have high hopes for that report. As with the previous ones, it will be a mixed picture. I have the impression that Blix will now be more negative than he was before, with regard to the Iraqis' intentions. After the appearance of the inspectors before the Council, we must anticipate a vote on the resolution one week later. The Iraqis, meanwhile, will try to explain that they are fulfilling their obligations. It isn't true, and it won't be sufficient, though they may announce the destruction of some missiles.

Bush: This is like Chinese water torture. We must put an end to it.
Aznar: I agree, but it would be good to have the maximum possible number of people. Have a little patience.

Bush: My patience is exhausted. I don't intend to wait longer than the middle of March.

Aznar: I do not request that you have infinite patience. Simply that you do everything possible so that it all works out.

Bush: Countries like Mexico, Chile, Angola, and Cameroon must realize that what's at stake is the security of the United States, and they should act with a sense of friendship toward us. [Chilean President Ricardo] Lagos should know that the Free Trade Accord with Chile is awaiting Senate confirmation and a negative attitude about this could put ratification in danger. Angola is receiving Millennium Account funds [to help alleviate poverty] and that could be jeopardized also if he's not supportive. And Putin must know that his attitude is putting in danger the relations of Russia with the United States.

Aznar: Tony [Blair] would like to wait until the 14th of March.

Bush: I prefer the 10th. This is like a game of bad cop, good cop. I don't mind being the bad cop, and Blair can be the good one.

Aznar: Is it certain that any possibility exists that Saddam Hussein will go into exile?

Bush: The possibility exists, including that he will be assassinated.

Aznar: Exile with a guarantee?

Bush: No guarantee. He is a thief, a terrorist, a war criminal. Compared with Saddam, Milosevic would be a Mother Teresa. When we go in, we are going to discover many more crimes and we will take him to the Court of International Justice. Saddam Hussein thinks that he has already escaped. He thinks that France and Germany have ceased fulfilling their responsibilities. He also thinks that the demonstrations of the last week [Saturday 15 February] will protect him. And he thinks that I am very weak. But the people around him know that things are otherwise. They know that his future is in exile or a coffin. For that reason it is very important to maintain the pressure on him. Gaddafi tells us through back channels that that is the only thing that can finish him off. Saddam Hussein's only strategy is to delay, to delay and to delay.

Aznar: In fact the biggest success would be to win the game without firing a single shot and entering Baghdad.
Bush: For me it would be the perfect solution. I do not want war. I know what wars are. I know the destruction and the death that they bring with them. I am the one who has to console the mothers and the widows of the dead. By all means, for us that would be the best solution. In addition, it would save $50 billion.

Aznar: We need you to help us with our public opinion.

Bush: We will do everything we can. Wednesday I am going to speak on the situation in the Middle East, proposing the new peace plan with which you are familiar, and on weapons of mass destruction, on the benefits of a free society, and I will locate the history of Iraq in a wider context. Perhaps it will serve you.

Aznar: What we are doing is a very deep change for Spain and the Spaniards. We are changing the policy that the country has followed for the past two hundred years.

Bush: A historical sense of responsibility guides me just as it does you. When within a few years history judges us, I do not want people to ask themselves why Bush, or Aznar, or Blair did not face their responsibilities. In the end, what people want is to enjoy freedom. Recently, in Romania, they reminded me of the example of Ceaușescu: it was enough for a woman to call him a liar, for the entire repressive edifice to come down. It is the uncontrollable power of freedom. I am convinced that I will get the resolution.

Aznar: All to the good.

Bush: I made the decision to go to the Security Council. In spite of the disagreements in my Administration, I said to my people that we had to work with our friends. It will be wonderful to get a second resolution.

Aznar: The only thing that worries me about you is your optimism.

Bush: I am optimistic because I believe that I am in the right. I am at peace with myself. It has been up to us to face a serious threat to the peace. It irritates me a great deal to consider the indifference of the Europeans to the sufferings that Saddam Hussein inflicts on Iraqis. Perhaps because he is brown-skinned, far away, and Muslim, many Europeans think that everything is all right in his regard. I will not forget what Solana once said to me: why do we Americans think that the Europeans are anti-Semitic and unable to confront their responsibilities? That defensive attitude is terrible. I have to acknowledge I have just great relations with Kofi Annan.

Aznar: He shares your ethical preoccupations.

Bush: The more the Europeans attack me, the stronger I am in the United States.
Aznar: We would like to make your strength compatible with the esteem of the Europeans.

WHAT OSAMA BIN LADEN SAID

When Osama Bin Laden's first video tape in three years was reported in September 2007, enormous press coverage was devoted to how his beard had changed colour, but it was almost impossible to find what he actually said. Eventually, al Jazeera published excerpts, some of which are reproduced here.

'At first, I say that despite the fact America possesses the greatest economic power and the most powerful and modern military arsenal, despite spending on this war much more than what the entire world spends on its armies, and despite it being the superpower influencing world policies – as if it has a monopoly on the unjust veto right – despite all of this, and with God's help, nineteen young men were able to change the direction of its compass ...

Bush mentions his co-operation with Maliki and his government to spread freedom in Iraq but, in fact, he is co-operating with the leaders of one sect against another sect, believing that this will lead him to a quick victory. Thus, he spread the so-called civil war, and things worsened in his hands and got out of his control ...

These are some facts pertaining to the freedom he says he is spreading. Bush's insistence not to give the United Nations an expanded mandate in Iraq is an implicit admission of his loss and defeat over there.

Amongst the most important items in Bush's speeches since September 11 is his statement that the Americans have no options but to continue the war. Such statements are in fact a repetition of the words of the neo-conservatives, such as Cheney, Rumsfeld and Richard Perle, who said earlier that the Americans have no option but to continue war, or to face a holocaust ... However, we are a people who do not tolerate oppression, we reject humiliation and disgrace, and we take revenge on the people of tyranny and aggression. The blood of the Muslims will not be spilled in vain, and the morrow is nigh for he who awaits ... The genocide of peoples and their holocaust was perpetrated on your hands. All what is left from the Red Indians is a few specimens. A short while ago, the Japanese observed the 62nd anniversary of the annihilation of Nagasaki and Hiroshima with your nuclear bombs ...

Yet, in spite of that, you [American citizens] allowed Bush to complete his first term. And what is even stranger is that you still chose him for a second term. This was a clear and explicit mandate you gave him, with your full knowledge and consent, to continue killing our people in Iraq and Afghanistan. Then you claim to be innocent. This innocence of yours is similar to my innocence of the blood of your sons on the 11th, were I to claim such a thing. But it is impossible to humour many of you in the arrogance and indifference you show for the lives of humans outside America, or to humour your leaders in lying. The whole world knows that they have the lion's share of that ...

In answer to the questions about the reasons for the Democrats' failure to stop the war, I say that these are the same reasons of the failure of former President [John] Kennedy to stop the Vietnam war. Those who possess real power and influence are the ones who have the biggest capital. And since the Democratic regime allows the major corporations to support candidates, be they presidential or congressional, then there should be no need for astonishment at the Democrats' failure to stop the war. You are the ones who say 'money talks'.

I also want to bring to your attention that among the greatest reasons for the collapse of the Soviet Union was their being afflicted with their leader [Leonid] Brezhnev, who was dominated by pride and arrogance and refused to recognise the facts on the ground. Since the first year of Afghanistan's invasion, reports indicated that the Russians were losing the war. However, he refused to admit this so that it would not be added as a defeat in his personal history – even though refusing to acknowledge defeat not only fails to change the truth for the wise ones, but also exacerbates the problem and increases the losses.

How similar is your situation today to their situation about two decades ago? The mistakes of Brezhnev are being committed by Bush. When asked about the date of withdrawing his troops from Iraq, he said that the withdrawal will not take place during his term, but during the term of his successor. The significance of these words is not hidden.'

Reviews

Bright-Eyed Shelley

Ann Wroe, *Being Shelley: The Poet's Search for Himself*, Jonathan Cape, 452 pages, ISBN 9780224080781, £25

Shelley, it seems, was not only the poet of the 'Ode to Liberty', 'Ode to the West Wind', 'To a Skylark', 'Prometheus Unbound' and much else; the political activist of Paul Foot's *Red Shelley*, responding to the Peterloo massacre with the 'Mask of Anarchy' and writing an 'Address to the Irish People' in revolt; nor was he just the atheist of the 'Necessity of Atheism', for which he was expelled from Oxford, disinherited by his father, deprived of the custody of his children, and forced into exile in Italy. Nor was he only the lover of five beautiful and very young women by whom he had several children, co-author in effect with his wife, Mary Wollstonecraft, of *Frankenstein,* and bosom friend of Byron. At Eton he was 'mad Shelley' because of his pranks with fireworks, a passion with pyrotechnics he persisted in throughout his short life in electrical and chemical experiments and even in dabbling with alchemy.

Shelley's scientific interests, however, were serious – in his studies of the works of Holbach and Humphrey Davy – and practically applied in his hydraulic work on the reclamation of land from the sea at Tremadoc in North Wales. He was a considerable linguist, making translations not only from the Italian, but from French, Spanish, Latin and ancient Greek. His education at Eton, from which he was twice expelled, embraced both the classics and sciences. On top of all this he liked to sail small boats in storms and heavy seas, which led inevitably to his early death at 30.

Who then was Shelley? This is the quest upon which Ann Wroe has embarked in her new book, deliberately entitled *Being Shelley: the Poet's Search for Himself*. In the blurb she writes,

> 'Four questions consumed Shelley and coloured everything he wrote. Who or what was he? What was his purpose? Where had he come from? And where was he going? He sought the answers in order to free and empower not only himself, but the whole human race. His revolution would shatter the earth's illusions, shock men and women with new visions, find true Love and Liberty – and take everyone with him.'

To put this passionate and radical quest at the centre of Shelley's life, Ann Wroe has drawn entirely on his known writings, trawling not only his published work in poetry and prose, letters and recorded conversations, but especially his notebooks preserved in the Bodleian Library at Oxford and the Huntingdon Library in San Merino, California.

The book does not take the form of a chronological biography, but, as Wroe insists, 'takes seriously Shelley's statement that a poet "participates in the eternal, the infinite and the one; as far as relates to his conceptions, time and place and number are not". Its narrative track is the poet's quest for truth through the steadily rarefying elements of earth, water, air and fire.' It is thus divided into four parts, Earth, Water, Air and Fire, each taking about 60 pages. These are then subdivided into chapters, which give the book a certain chronological sequence, but allow the author to capture the continuity of Shelley's thinking – his quest for truth, beauty, liberty and love – throughout his life.

Earth is where he comes from – his youth, heritage, disinheritance, marriages, debts, exile, an outcast, but with a spirit behind the mask.

Water is where he belongs – on the Thames at Marlowe, on Lake Geneva, in the Bay of Livorno, but also in his dreams, under water and in the reflections of the mind as a mirror of the 'wide sea of misery', whose ripples lead inexorably to death.

Air is the power that carries him up from the earth and water into the clouds and mountain tops, that gives him his songs and rushes him forward on the wind so that his poetry survives. 'Orpheus, torn to pieces, still made music.'

Fire is what literally fires him, in the fireworks and alchemy, the haunting human spirit overcoming evil and even death. As in Plato's *Phaedrus*, the soul passes on at death to universal love, mind is one infinitesimal part of the One Mind. In his Adonais, it is 'The Light which kindles the Universe ... the fire for which all thirst ... Consuming the clouds of cold mortality.'

The book begins and ends with the fatal voyage in the Ligurian Sea with his friend Edward Williams.

So, what kind of life was lost by Shelley's impetuosity and suicidal tendencies? The first answer must be a spirit of extra-ordinary vitality, swept, the only appropriate word, by a power throughout his life, which he firmly rejected as Spinoza's definition of God. What he did concede is that:

> 'There is a power by which we are surrounded, like the atmosphere in which some motionless lyre is suspended, which visits us with its *breath* (his emphasis) our silent chords at will, and those who have seen God, have, in the period of their purer and more perfect nature, been harmonised by their own will, to so exquisite [a] consentaneity of powers, as to give forth divinest melody when the breath of universal being sweeps over their frame.'

It has to be said that there are moments in his meanderings, and the crossing out of words and lines in his drafts of poems, when it seems as if the laudanum, which he started to imbibe at Eton, had taken over, rather than any 'motionless lyre'.

Shelley was a mass of contradictions. He carried pistols, was a good shot and used them, but opposed political violence. He told Leigh Hunt, when talking of reform, 'I am one of those whom nothing will fully satisfy' but, by 1815, he told his wife Mary, he had 'begun to feel that the time for action was not yet ripe in England and that the pen was the only instrument wherewith to prepare the way for better things'. He could cheer revolutions – in Spain, Naples and Greece – but, unlike his friend Byron, could not 'push them forward'. He was a vegetarian. Byron feared that, if his illegitimate daughter were brought up by the Shelleys, as they proposed, she would 'perish of starvation and green fruit'. Some of his friends thought his diet made him nervous, weak and fanciful, 'lightness', as Wroe comments, 'being escape from the flesh'. In 1816, he was weighing his daily food intake. But he could be found feasting on bacon and veal chops well-peppered and shot game in England, and caught fish to eat in Italy.

Wroe sums up his politics:

> 'The pragmatic reformer, the stirrer of minds and the enthusiast for associations were only three aspects of his political self. There was always another, burning, waiting, for the moment when other means seemed hopeless. His writings were meant to start destroying and purifying fires, the words searing individually into minds and hearts and igniting, he hoped, a roaring chain reaction.'

Hunt saw him as one of Milton's rebel angels holding a 'reed tipt with fire', about to unloose Satan's whole artillery against the host of Heaven. Wroe quotes Shelley's *Revolt of Islam* where he sees the planet Venus, the Morning Star, blazing on the brow of her daemon lover. Kissing her tenderly, breathing a 'wild dissolving bliss' through her body, he urged her to fight for liberty and truth, as if he were Milton's Lucifer luring away the angels to follow his defiance – or, as Wroe adds, 'as if he were Shelley, bright eyed, loving and subversive' – Lucifer the devil but also the light bearer, like Shelley.

Shelley himself must have the last word:

> 'For the poet not only beholds intensely the present as it is, and discovers those laws according to which present things ought to be ordered, but he beholds the future in the present, and his thoughts are the germs of the flower and the fruit of latest time.'

As he ends his 'Prometheus Unbound', where 'man' must be read to encompass men and women equally, which Goethe's Faust had inspired and for which Shelley's experiments in alchemy had suggested the worship and liberation of the discoverer of fire, bound seemingly for ever to the rocky earth, in the air above the waters;

> *The loathsome mask has fallen, the man remains*
> *Sceptreless, free, uncircumscribed, but man*
> *Equal, unclassed, tribeless and nationless,*
> *Exempt from awe, worship, degree, the king*
> *Over himself ...*

Michael Barratt Brown

More Time for Benn

Tony Benn, selected and edited by Ruth Winstone, *More Time for Politics, Diaries 2001-2007*, Hutchinson, 352 pages, ISBN 9780091920562, £20

Many people thought that *Free at Last* would be the last volume of Tony Benn's extraordinary diaries, which had covered a lifetime in Parliament, and eleven years as a Cabinet Minister. In those far off days, Tony Benn was a member of the Labour Party's National Executive, and firmly, indeed permanently, fixed in the public eye. Leaving Parliament in May 2001, he might have been expected to enter a period of retirement, resting on his abundant laurels.

But this latest volume records a life of amazing activity, which lives up to the injunction of his wife, Caroline, that leaving Parliament behind would allow him to express himself more fully, with *More Time for Politics*, as he has entitled the work.

I was going to say that this would be the last of the Benn memoirs: but apparently, not so. He is already planning the new sequel, and burning up the miles in his campaigns, which will no doubt find their way into the forthcoming volume, as yet unwritten.

Ruth Winstone tells us that this volume is 'perhaps the most candid' of all that have appeared so far. She has enjoyed editing it for that reason. I found it poignant and at times deeply moving. The death of Caroline brought about a fearful bereavement, which continued to hurt more as the months turned into years. Benn describes himself as driving to Stansgate, sobbing deeply all the way. His grief is palpable and continuous, and perhaps helps to explain his demonic energy as a campaigner.

Shortly after this book was published, he was rising up at 5.00 a.m. to attend a rally of postmen, who were embattled in their recent strike. No doubt his appearance among them would have been a great encouragement. Equally without doubt, there is no other prominent Labour leader who is worth a flicker of support by workers in the postal services, in the unlikely event that they might tentatively offer sympathy in their struggle. The great mystery is how the postmen's leaders have been able to sustain their Union's affiliation to the Labour Party through the rain of blows which it has showered on their members.

But of course, a vast proportion of Benn's efforts, as monitored in detail in these Diaries, concerns the wars in Iraq and elsewhere, and the struggle against them. We thus have a detailed account of the circumstances leading up to the visit to Saddam Hussein, and of the subsequent interview with the Iraqi President on the very eve of the Anglo-American invasion. The dictator told the truth in response to Benn's questions. There were no weapons of mass destruction. But there were plenty of weapons of mass destruction about to fall on Baghdad during the Shock and Awe offensive which was immediately to follow.

Benn describes his interview with an official of the Iraqi Government, Dr. Amir Al Saadi, who was head of the Ministry responsible for weapons of mass destruction, and for negotiations with the Inspectors. Al Saadi was a very convincing witness, who stuck very closely to the scientific evidence. He told Benn of earlier attempts to withhold information from Hans Blix, at the time that he had directed the International Atomic Energy Agency. This experience had persuaded Blix to be extremely cautious about accepting Iraqi protestations. But 'Al Saadi told me that there had been one hundred per cent eradication in 1992 of their whole nuclear programme, all done under the supervision of the IAEA'.

I never met Al Saadi myself, but I did watch him carefully on CNN, when his extensive interviews were televised. I found him a most persuasive witness. Subsequently I read in the press that, after the invasion, Al Saadi had given himself up to the coalition forces. He had figured in the pack of cards of Iraqi leaders meriting instant arrest. That is how he found himself in prison at Baghdad airport, held in seclusion and extensively debriefed. I began a campaign to secure his release from prison, and we gathered the support of a number of political leaders, across Party boundaries, together with a variety of journalists and lawyers. Tony himself wrote to Jack Straw about the case, and received a reasonable response. But it took an inordinately long while to secure Al Saadi's release, in spite of the fact that the German Government pressed for it, because Mrs. Al Saadi was also a German citizen.

Naturally, these Diaries are full of demonstrations, rallies in Trafalgar Square, and high profile public events. At one point, Benn, exhausted by marching round the town, asks a police horseman for a lift, and is told that he can have one, if he can climb on the horse. He ruefully admits that this task was beyond him, but tells us that it would have been a splendid entry to the demonstration, had it only come about.

But if this is a small part of the politics for which he had more time, there is still quite a lot of time spent on politics of the conventional kind. Part of this flows from his affection for Parliamentary institutions, which ensured that he was given free access to the Palace of Westminster on his retirement. He records his gratitude to the Speaker, Michael Martin, who gave him the Freedom of the House. Evidently, this was very useful, and was indeed heavily used.

The Parliamentary connection goes a long way to explaining the remarkable affection which seems to have grown up between Tony Benn and Ted Heath, and his ability to get on with political opponents. But most people will find the stories which exemplify this fact to be less perplexing than the powerful affinities of family, which make the hammer of Blair and Blairism so unaffectedly proud of the progress of his son, Hilary, up the Parliamentary greasy pole. Of course, he remembers his own progress, and knows better than anyone the difficulties which attended it. And of course, Hilary has been a considerable success in the New Labour Government. But this is a New Labour success, which must surely occasion some mixture of feelings in someone who was so unambiguously typical of the old Labour Party.

Tony Benn has left it to other people to make judgements on all such questions. This book is a masterly editorial labour. It succeeds brilliantly in presenting the real opinions of Benn as they have actually been, unvarnished, unmediated, and certainly unexpurgated. It makes me proud to have known the man whose life it records.

Ken Coates

Regime Change in Iran?

Scott Ritter, *Target Iran: The Truth about the White House's Plans for Regime Change,* **Politico's Publishing, 2006, 256 pages, ISBN 9781842751972, £16.99**

Scott Ritter's detailed, thorough analysis of how the Iran crisis has escalated to the point of intense fear of another war in the Gulf could hardly come at a better time.

Ritter, the former UN weapons inspector in Iraq, whose prognosis of the deceit being perpetrated by the US and UK governments with allegations of Iraq's weapons of mass destruction proved correct on every single count, has written this book as a way to warn how another policy of regime change is been sold to the public under the nominal guise of concern over illicit weapons.

What Ritter brings out from the start of the book that many other commentators have shied away from discussing is the extensive role of Israel in the build-up of hostilities. The confrontation between the United States and Iran is, according to Ritter, a 'conflict born in Israel', as Israel perceives Iran as the main strategic challenger to its military dominance of the Middle East. Drawing upon his own familiarity with key Israeli military and intelligence officials, developed during his time as an inspector in Iraq, Ritter shows how Israeli officials and their lobbyists in the United States brought the issue onto the international news agenda from 2002. They continued to stress, with claims that are dubious at best, the danger – in the preferred terminology of the moment, the 'existential danger' – that Iran poses to Israel.

Ritter describes how Israeli lobby groups in the United States, particularly the American-Israeli Public Affairs Committee (AIPAC), have tried to steer US policy on Iran. AIPAC's annual conference in March 2007 turned into anti-Iran rally, with speaker after speaker calling for the United States to harden its policy on Iran. Troublingly, senior US Democrats tried to outflank the Bush administration at the conference by calling for a more aggressive approach. The willingness of the Democrat-controlled Congress to curtail the Bush's administrations plans is seriously in doubt. In a speech to a US pro-Democrat think-tank in February, Nicholas Burns, the third ranking official in the State Department, called Iran 'the most disruptive, negative force in the Middle East'. Al Qaeda, it seems, are old hat for Burns. Blaming Iran for the disaster in Iraq has become standard fare in US policy circles.

In fact, Iran has repeatedly attempted to reach a negotiated compromise with the United States. These offers have been rebuffed, most notably Vice-President Cheney's dismissal of Iran's 2003 proposal for an all-encompassing bargain that traded off Iran's nuclear programme for an end to US-led sanctions. Iran's compliance with international nuclear inspections has been ignored by the United States, which has instead just raised the threshold for what it takes as compliance.

By mixing the politics of regime change in Iran with that of nuclear non-proliferation, Iranian concessions on nuclear issues have been made unlikely: Iran is not going to remove the nuclear option if it thinks the United States is trying to bring its government down, weapons or no weapons. One effect of US inflexibility has been the rise of the radicals within the Iranian political establishment: Mahmoud Ahmedinejad's victory in the 2005 presidential election came on the back of well-known US attempts to foment discontent within Iran.

Ritter speculates persuasively that this was part of a policy not of miscalculation but of intentional provocation. His views on this receive confirmation from a speech of John Bolton, United States ambassador to the UN until he was ousted in December 2006. Bolton told an AIPAC meeting a month later that he had hoped that Iran would throw the weapons inspectors out of the country, because 'that kind of reaction would produce a counter-reaction that actually would be more beneficial to us'. In other words, what matters to the Bush administration is not the extent to which Iran's nuclear programme is contained, but the degree to which the United States can manoeuvre Iran into a position of international isolation, and military action against it can take place.

Nevertheless, what could the United States actually do against Iran? Ritter, for one, thinks the prospect of sustained US military action against Iran is likely. The US moved two aircraft carriers into the Gulf in an overt display of hostility. A spate of articles in recent months has considered the prospect of US or Israeli airstrikes against Iran, with the purpose of destroying nuclear sites there. These articles have mostly been fed by briefings from within the US administration, and are likely to be disinformation, trying to cause fear within the Iranian administration rather than genuine accounts of policy. Iran's nuclear sites cannot be destroyed by airstrikes, and the only regimes to be destabilised by them would be those of US allies in the Muslim world.

But the raising of tensions, the deepening of US sanctions against Iran, and the increased attempts by the United States to cast the conflict with Iran in sectarian terms – pulling a group of Sunni-led states in the Arab world into a coalition against Shi'a Iran – are all highly dangerous and provocative. The prospects for conflict are very real, even if the Bush administration does not intend it at the moment. *Target Iran* shows us not only how we have arrived at this situation, but also what is happening within the US and Israeli governments that could turn the present crisis into an all-out war.

Glen Rangwala
with grateful acknowledgements to Palestine News

The First Holocaust

Taner Aksam, *A Shameful Act: The Armenian Genocide and the Question of Turkish Responsibility*, Constable, 496 pages, ISBN 9781845295523, £9.99

Although the deaths of some one-and-a-half million Armenian citizens of the Ottoman Empire, during the First World War, have been condemned as genocide by most authorities who have studied what occurred, the official Turkish position is that, despite the fact that the events were tragic, they were an unintended result of the war, for which the Armenians themselves bore major responsibility. The assassination in January 2007 of Hrant Dink, a Turkish citizen of Armenian descent who challenged this view, highlights the passions which the issue continues to generate in Turkey down to the present time. Hrant Dink, a journalist, was regarded by Turkish nationalists as a traitor and, before he was brutally murdered, received numerous threats against his life for denouncing the Armenian massacres.

In 1987, the European Parliament approved a resolution which called upon the Turkish Government to acknowledge the fact that the Armenian massacres were genocide. As a Member of the European Parliament who spoke out in support of the resolution, I was left in no doubt about the strength of Turkish opposition to it. Letters, leaflets, pamphlets and books putting the Turkish case were showered on MEPs as part of a sustained campaign designed to secure the defeat of the resolution. This was not successful, but it meant that it was a hard fight to achieve a majority in favour of the resolution, as many MEPs were undoubtedly influenced by the Turkish onslaught.

Personally, I was convinced of the Armenian case by a huge volume of evidence which cannot be refuted by the Turkish arguments – the Memoirs of Henry Morgenthau, US Ambassador at Constantinople 1913-16; documents presented to Viscount Grey of Falloden by Viscount Bryce; Christopher Walker: *The Survival of a Nation*; the hearings of the Permanent People's Tribunal on the Armenian Genocide, held in Paris in 1984; together with a host of other documents and books, provide an incontestable account of the facts that no contrary arguments can possibly nullify. There were, undoubtedly, attempts by Armenian elements to stir up rebellion against the Ottoman Empire and some committed brutal and inhumane acts. These were not, however, characteristic of the Armenian population of Anatolia as a whole and in no way could they possibly justify the genocidal policies implemented by Ottoman leaders during the First World War.

A Shameful Act by Taner Aksam is the first example of an exhaustive study by a Turkish expert which condemns the mass killings as genocide. The book brings forward new evidence to support the arguments of those who contend they were the result of a deliberate policy conceived and implemented by leading members of the Ottoman Government.

The new evidence has been extracted from the records of extraordinary courts martial set up by the Ottoman Government which came to power after the surrender of 1918. In an effort to dissociate itself from the massacres and curry favour at the Paris Peace Conference the new government sought to place responsibility on Talat Pasha, Enver Pasha and Cemal Pasha, the leaders of the Committee of Union and Progress (C.U.P), which was the ruling party during the war years. Sixty-three courts martial, including those of the wartime cabinet members, took place and evidence was provided by top Ottoman army commanders and high ranking officials, amongst others, which made it clear that the massacres had been centrally planned and implemented by a Special Organisation formed for the purpose which recruited former convicts, recent immigrants from the Caucasus and Rumelia, and some Kurds to carry out the killings.

The reason why the documents have not been previously used is that they have been vigorously 'pruned' and scattered, and they are written in Turkish in an Arabic script, which can be read by comparatively few scholars. Significant portions have, furthermore, not come to light.

This book makes it clear that, after the defeats of the Balkan Wars of 1912 and 1913 had led to the loss of 60 per cent of the Ottoman Empire's European territories, there was a desperate fear in certain ruling circles of the possible break-up of the Turkish homeland in Anatolia. Here, a third of the population was Christian – Armenians, Greeks, Assyrians and others – peoples who had no common identity with the Moslem majority. If the Armenians split away in the east and Greeks in the Aegean region in the west, the integrity of Anatolia would be fundamentally breached and the possibility of links with Turkish peoples in Central Asia destroyed. Leading Turkish nationalists were prepared to be ruthless in the extreme to get rid of the alien population

Secret meetings were held in the Ministry of War, then under the control of Enver Pasha, in May, June and August 1914 to work out plans to force the Greeks to leave. In 1918 it was estimated that between 300,000 and half a million had been evicted from Thrace and hundreds of thousands had died. Action against the Greeks was followed by an even more systematic process to eliminate the Armenians. The Armenian genocide is said to have begun on 24 April 1915. On 24 May, the Ottoman Government reported that 2,345 people had been arrested in Istanbul. Between May and August 1915, the bulk of the Armenian population in the eastern provinces was deported and murdered *en masse*.

Taner Aksam gives a detailed account of the massacres and quotes telegrams presented at the courts martial, which suggest that Dr. Barhaettim Sakir Bey, the chief of the Special Organisation was, in effect, the director of the massacres. Some provincial governors refused to accept the orders sent to them and some were murdered as a result of their obstinacy. The documents leave no doubt, Taner Aksam states, that Talat Pasha was the over all co-ordinator of the deportations and massacres, although he sent some duplicitous telegraphs referring to humane treatment.

The charge of genocide of the Armenian people is confirmed and underpinned by this book which is – most unusually – the work of a Turkish authority. After the Treaty of Sèvres of 10 August 1920, which proposed to create an Armenian state in eastern Anatolia, the courts martial ceased. A nationalist wave led by Kemal Mustafa (Ataturk) swept the country and Turkish responsibility for the massacres was vociferously denied – as it has been, officially, ever since. It was felt that any concession on this issue would greatly have weakened the case for ignoring the Treaty of Sèvres and refusing to accept the establishment of an Armenian State in eastern Anatolia.

However, as Taner Aksam points out, the continuing refusal on the part of the Turkish Government and its people to accept responsibility for the massacres cannot be justified by a blatant refusal to accept the facts. These are set forth in the detailed and expert study which yet again confirms the conclusions reached by other dispassionate scholars. There can be no doubt that the treatment meted out to its Armenian citizens by the Turkish leaders during the First World War constitutes genocide.

If the possibility of further genocidal massacres is to be minimised, it is vital that there should be no cover-up and the Turkish authorities today must accept this sooner or later. Furthermore, those of us who believe in the importance of human rights must never back down on the issue.

The author's courage matches the high quality of his scholarship. This is a very important book and all who believe in international justice and the cause of human rights should read it with care. The Armenian massacres are not an issue of concern to historians alone. They continue to have a vital contemporary relevance which must not be ignored.

Stan Newens

Understanding the Anti-Slavers

Adam Hochschild, *Bury the Chains: The British Struggle to Abolish Slavery,* Pan Books, 2006, 468 pages, ISBN 978-0330485814, £8.99

In concluding his introduction to this book, Adam Hochschild quotes the social anthropologist, Margaret Mead: 'Never doubt that a small group of thoughtful, committed citizens can change the world. Indeed, it is the only thing that ever has'. One such change, the ending of the slave trade, took place, Hochschild's book demonstrates convincingly, as the result, after no more than a life-time's campaigning, of a meeting in the late afternoon of 22 May 1787 at 2 George Yard in the City of London, of twelve men, several of them Quakers, determined to launch a campaign. The date is important, just after the American Revolution and just before the French, neither of which proposed the abolition of slavery, though they certainly encouraged slave revolts.

The success of this campaign has to be set against the enormity of the change that was proposed. The division of societies into slave and free was at that time generally accepted as natural. All previous civilisations were built on slavery – Greek, Roman, Chinese, Indian, Arabian, Aztec. The British, French, Russian and recent American empires were no different. At the end of the Eighteenth Century, Hochschild claims, well over three-quarters of the world's peoples were in some form of bondage. The campaign in Britain, moreover, came up against not only the power of the plantation owners and ship owners, who were well represented in an unreformed Parliament, but against a ruling class that regarded all dissident voices, and especially organised ones, as seditious and even traitorous in the war against France.

Hochschild has researched in depth the writings and activities of the anti-slavery campaigners. In the story he tells, Thomas Clarkson emerges as a heroic figure, several times threatened with assassination, devoting a 16 hour day to the campaign, travelling on horseback in all some 35,000 miles, as Hochschild puts it, 'from waterfront pubs to an audience with an emperor, from the decks of navy ships to parliamentary hearing rooms', flooding Parliament with petitions signed by thousands, organising a boycott of slave grown sugar which 300,000 Britons supported, distributing leaflets and posters, describing the horrendous treatment of African men and women, with drawings of their actual imprisonment cheek by jowl on the slave ships.

Other heroes emerge from the story – Granville Sharp, a musician, pamphleteer and pioneer anti-slavery crusader; John Newton, ex-slave ship captain and later abolitionist; Olaudaur Equiano, whose autobiography introduced thousands of Britons to the life of a slave, who earned his freedom; and, of course, William Wilberforce, who introduced bills in Parliament over four decades. Wilberforce remains by far the best known of the abolitionists. This honour is very unfair to Clarkson in particular, especially since Wilberforce was only concerned with the abolition of the slave trade, not of slavery itself, and opposed the slave revolts. It may be added that Wilberforce was also the man who to save the 'poor benighted heathen' had missionaries sent to India, which, according to William Dalrymple, reviewing in *The Guardian* (25.08.07) the British Museum's current exhibition of Indian art, ended the period of cultural fraternisation between British colonial officials and Hindoos.

An important question which Hochschild raises is how it could come about that it was in Britain and nowhere else that the struggle to abolish slavery took place – in a Britain, moreover, that was building a vast empire and stood to lose most from abolition. Hochschild gives an estimate of a loss of 1.8 per cent of Britain's national income over more than half a century. He suggests three explanations. The first was that the abolitionists developed for the first time a whole range of campaigning tools that have become standard for all subsequent campaigners on other issues: centralised control of regional and local activities, with lists of supporters, lobbying, Parliamentary hearings and petitions, supported by leaflets, posters, newspaper articles, advertisements, cartoons and books, public meetings, demonstrations, consumer boycotts, investigative reporting, slogans and logos and buttons to wear (Wedgwood designed one showing a black man in chains with the surrounding words: 'Am I not a man and a brother?').

That such propaganda was effective depended on Hochschild's second argument – the increase of literacy in Britain and the enormous expansion of publishing in the late Eighteenth Century. It is significant that the first meeting of the abolitionists was in a London printing shop. There were a dozen newspapers published in London in the mid-1780s, most of them dailies, and 49 newspapers elsewhere in Britain and dozens of magazines. Coach travel was growing rapidly with a regular royal mail. By the 1780s more than half the population could read and write, judging by entries in Parish registers. Britain was far ahead of other countries in these respects. The sheer quantity of books published is amazing, particularly by non-conformist churches which were strong supporters of abolition. The Methodist Book Room in London distributed its literature 'by the ton'.

None of this would have been enough to ensure the success of the abolitionists' campaign, if there had not been a wide measure of sympathy for the cause. That this existed at all in an imperial Britain extending white rule over millions of blacks world-wide must be surprising. Hochschild is able to identify, most interestingly, one single factor (and this is his third explanation) that created that sympathy – impressments into the Royal Navy. No inhabitant of London, Liverpool, Bristol or any other British port could walk safely in the streets during the Napoleonic wars without fear of being forcibly seized and marched off by the press gangs. The comparison with African men and women seized in their villages for transport across the Atlantic to work on the slave plantations was only too close. Pictures of black men and women huddled together in the slave ships evoked a natural reaction that such a fate could await even the most peaceful Englishman going about his daily business. There were no slaves in Britain, apart from wage slaves, and they were confused enough by their apparent market freedom to feel no need to oppose the bondage of others.

This is a long book and fully referenced, but it makes a very good read with many fascinating insights into the nature of the slave trade and conditions on the slave plantations and into the political economy of Britain at the end of the Eighteenth and beginning of the Nineteenth Century. And Hochschild does not fail to make the comparison between the situation of the abolitionists then and movements for social change today. It seems now for most people that world-wide inequalities are only natural and that exploitation of the earth's carbon deposits for private transport by car and plane can go on for ever. All the tools and means for campaigning on such issues are more available than ever with the spread of the internet. There exist here and there many small groups of thoughtful and committed citizens engaged in the relevant campaigns. But who is listening? What could take the place of the press gangs, which would unite people's sense of solidarity without exacerbating their fear of reprisals?

Michael Barratt Brown

Australia's Genocide

Sven Lindqvist, *Terra Nullius: A Journey Through No One's Land*, Granta Books, 256 pages, ISBN 9781862078956, £10

This text is unique and merits the encomium printed on the cover of the English edition. Quoting Phillip Knightley, author of *Australia: A Biography of a Nation*, the cover informs readers they are about to read 'the most original work on Australia and its treatment of Aboriginals they have ever read'. Its originality lies in the insights and challenging ideas it presents. The bibliography is impressive; so, too, is his critique of earlier intellectual luminaries such as Marx, Durkheim, Kropotkin, Freud, Malinowski, and Alfred Radcliffe-Brown. All sought to understand the social structure and beliefs of the Aborigines.

Lindqvist takes up this challenge and presents his case in the form of a travelogue as he drives through the Northern Territory and Western Australia. Some, including your reviewer, may be irritated by details of the topography, flora and fauna, the quality of his accommodation, and so on. His historical narrative relates to his major themes, rooted in Australia's penal past and enforced settlement, and enriches our understanding of the contemporary country.

Read as a travelogue, the text has little value. Australia is unique in containing major sections of its population who are out and out racists, and who reinforce their mindset by denying the appalling treatment of their indigenous neighbours. As in no other country, historiography is pursued with the intensity of a pit-bull terrier. In Britain historians contend, in Australia the debate is far more intense and abusive. In Australia, European occupation obliterated a people – in Tasmania the Aborigines were regarded as vermin and exterminated. Elsewhere in Australia it is estimated that nine-tenths of the population were overwhelmed. As Lindqvist documents, they were an inferior race doomed to 'fade away', following their contact with Western culture.

Australia has the equivalent of our home-grown holocaust denier, David Irvine. Keith Windshuttle, author of *The Fabrication of Aboriginal History*, claims that no genocide was committed – the massacres were legitimate police actions. He rejects practically everything academic historians have unearthed concerning Aboriginal history. He contends such evidence is a gigantic forgery, intended to deprive Australians of their right to be proud of their history.

Despite the welcome changes introduced by the Keating and Whitlam Governments, the changes in public sentiment and the calls for public figures to apologise for the conduct of their forebears, sections of Australian society refuse to recognise that the past is scarred by major embarrassments. In writing this I suspect that few readers are aware that it was not until 1962 that Aboriginal people acquired the right to vote in both State and Commonwealth elections. Unlike other public figures, John Howard has refused to apologise for the countless misdeeds of his forebears.

Many Australians see through the revisionist rhetoric of Windshuttle and his ilk and recognise they have a duty to apologise and say sorry for the conduct of their forebears. Lindqvist illustrates his point by giving an account of visiting Norway in 1951 where he was chastened for Sweden's collaboration with Nazi Germany in the early 1940s, despite the fact that he was then only ten. He asks: were his fellow Norwegians right to blame him? It is difficult to fault his reply. It should touch all of us; he insists that persons who over the years have benefited from the crimes of their forebears cannot avoid the burden of guilt. He concludes:

> 'When the misdeeds of the past are brought to light, when the perpetrators and their heirs confess and ask for forgiveness, when we do penance and mend our ways and pay the price – then the crime committed has a new setting and a new significance. No longer the inescapable extinction of a people, but its ability to survive and ultimately to have the justice of its claim acknowledged.'

This is a lesson that Australia has still to learn. To visit Australia without first reading *Terra Nullius* could make you a party to the past.

Peter M. Jackson

Shopping Abuse

Andrew Simms, ***Tescopoly: How one shop came out on top and why it matters***, **Constable, 372 pages, paperback ISBN 9781845295110, £7.99**

Thankfully this book is not solely about Tesco – rather, the author uses the brand largely for illustrative purposes to highlight the transformations that have occurred in retailing in general and the effects of these changes, both in local and global terms. Certainly Tesco is by far the dominant presence in grocery retailing in the United Kingdom and the book does, as one would expect, chart its growth both nationally and increasingly internationally. It details the tactics it has used, along with the other three major grocery retailers (Asda/Wal-Mart, Morrisons, Sainsbury's) to achieve their present oligopolistic position. It is a classic tale of neo-liberalist success which comes at a very high price at many different levels in both a global and local context. The book seeks to criticise modern retailing using a number of connected ideas but largely those of radical ecology, neo-Keynesian/ development economics, localism and the ideas of E.F.Schumacher: the author is in fact the present Policy Director of the New Economics Foundation (NEF).

The New Economics Foundation campaign on 'clone towns' and 'ghost-town Britain' fits neatly into the arguments propounded, and sees Tesco as leading the charge in the destruction of local shopping centres and local economies. Its record for sharp legal practice in forcing elected councils' aquiescence in the development of out-of-town superstores, often in the teeth of grassroots local community opposition, is documented thoroughly. The supermarkets are not restricted by planning 'red tape' beloved of *Daily Mail* editorials: they have the legal might to get what they want, and the landbank to ensure it's where they want. Tesco, of course, has the largest landbank, which is not merely for internal expansion, but also to restrict the opportunities of competitors.

The book recounts the demise of the local shopkeeper over the last 20 years and links it comparatively with the overall decrease in retail employment, despite the oft repeated reassurances to the contrary by the retail behemoths. The author is convinced that the new forms of chain retailing and brand marketing, largely developed in the United States, are destroying what little local community life remains, leaving us as atomised, solipsistic consumers in the confines of an Orwellian dystopia where the slogans do not yet claim 'war is peace' but do say 'helping you spend less every day'. It is true that community destruction owes much to the siting of out-of-town supermarkets with free parking and the one-stop nature of retail grocery: but we can also cite the manic juggling for many families of childcare, food preparation, domestic duties in general, not forgetting the requirement to put in the longest working hours in Europe. In fact, as the author points out, the name 'supermarket' is a bit of a misnomer. The supermarket is not a market at all, for a market requires ease of price comparison – you cannot check prices when you are physically isolated from competitors. When you are in Tesco you cannot check Asda's price equivalent three miles down the road. As Vance Packard made clear all those years ago, the retailer desires us to lose ourselves in the soothing balm of consumerist excess and dulling of comparative proclivities. For the author our communities, both urban and rural, are being destroyed not by the sameness and uniformity of a centrally planned East European economy, but by 'the reality of dreary market economies, centrally planned by corporations'. The development of Tesco is intimately associated with this process.

Tesco's historical rise from its small beginnings is repeatedly used as an example of innovation leading to success. The book charts the rise of monopolistic retailing both nationally and internationally and the Tesco story in particular: from its humble East End beginnings in 1919 to the Titan of today. It is perhaps not without some irony that a grocer's daughter from Grantham was to be the orchestrator of big capital's virtual annihilation of its cornershop competitor. One can only wonder at the possible consequences if Tesco's development had been a little more precocious! The chimera 'choice' so loved by Thatcher and her later prime-minsterial clones has become for Andrew Simms its very opposite, the very 'death of diversity' – from the constraints placed on suppliers concerning the norms of what constitutes the acceptability for a vegetable by supermarket buyers (tasteless, uniform in size, and blemish free) to the deliberate blandness of much supermarket food. Supermarket practice is the antithesis of diversity, which is visible more in the packaging and the marketing context. Even the Tesco buildings look the bloody same! Simms sees an anology between Darwinian evolutionary theory with its need for genetic diversity and the economic outcomes of the last 25 years under the neo-liberal economic dispensation. The freedom of markets, not to mention the striving to maximise capital's return, (a point which could have done with perhaps a little more emphasis in the book), has resulted in the very narrowing of diversity in opportunities, both social and economic. The vast majority of mankind is increasingly left with the mere appearance of diversity through consumerist product choice.

The supermarket experience is now in the process of being exported from its Western hemisphere homeland with all the major supermarket chains, Tesco being no exception, expanding in Eastern Europe and South-East Asia in particular. The 'clone town' is becoming an international reality, fed by ever-increasing Third World urbanisation and the continued destruction of the small family-based agricultural unit, subsistence or otherwise. The Third World still has millions of small farmers and, as the control of indigenous food sources is increasingly determined by the requirements of locally operating supermarkets, we can look forward to increasing diminution of local markets with its corollary, the consolidation of larger agriculture units with intensified labour exploitation and product mono-culture. The rates of suicide among small farmers within the Indian sub-continent and South Korea are a grim sign of the process at work.

The relationship between the supermarkets and their suppliers is dealt with in detail, although the facts are not easily obtained given the latter's fear of supermarket retribution for unsanctioned disclosure. In fact, a virtual Mafia-like *omertà* applies to relationships in this area with the retribution for infringement, naturally enough, the exclusion from the approved suppliers list. This situation is not helped by what the author considers a very light regulatory touch by the relevant government authorities, primarily the Office of Fair Trading (OFT) or, as it is more unkindly known, the Office in Favour of Tesco! The recent OFT bearing of its milk teeth over dairy price-fixing by the big four has yet to show blood and, of course, 'in separate statements, Asda, Tesco and Sainsbury's said they would vigorously defend themselves' *(Guardian 21/09/07)*.

Dare one say that the authorities' benign attitude to the supermarkets reflects New Labour's relationship with the retail giants, and Tesco in particular, which has been close, to say the least? Blair's pre-2001 election splutter at a public meeting about the supermarkets' 'armlock' on farmers was swiftly forgotten, as was Gordon Brown's earlier pledge to 'expose and end anti-competitive practices' in his 1999 'rip-off Britain' campaign. The connection between Tesco and New Labour has been particularly matey, with the former helping find timely millions for the Millennium Dome and the sharing of 'human resouces' in the form of Phillip Gould, Blair's one time policy advisor and court sycophant. Unsurprisingly, it seems we can expect little or no change in that close relationship from a Brown Government, with Sir Terry Leahy appointed to Brown's *Business Council for Britain,* along with such luminaries as Damon Buffini (hedge funds) and Alan Sugar (abrasive capitalism's human TV face). Neither does Brown seem unduly worried by Leahy's salary of £4.6 million with a proposed bonus of £10 million. Perhaps he now shares the views of his supposed, erstwhile foe, Peter Mandelson, and is 'intensely relaxed about people getting filthy rich'. One thing is certain – there's no danger of that if you are a shelf stacker at Tesco on £11,100 a year!

The labour force both nationally and internationally gets a pretty raw deal from Tesco and other supermarkets, and *Tescopoly* highlights much of the research many readers will already be familiar with. From banana growers in Honduras to garment workers in Sri Lanka, the price of cheap goods for Western markets is made clear with its attendant distortion of Third World economies and human exploitation. Within the context of the Third World, both the ideas of *Fair Trade* and *Food Sovereignty,* (the latter concerned with the rights of peoples and communities to decide on trading relationships outside their immediate locales), are touched upon. The detrimental environmental effects of supermarket retailing, again now sadly well-known to us all, are mentioned, and it is a testament to the effectiveness of books like this that all the chains have felt it necessary to wage their own 'greenwash' campaigns. The book does relate various fight-backs against supermarket expansion, and the proliferation of local group activities testifies to the strength of feeling against the new retailing, and successes have been recorded. The doughty citizens of Saxmundham have, so far, fought off a Tesco in their town, but they are unfortunately more the exception rather than the rule.

One failing of this terribly worthy book is that it has so little to say about Tesco's own UK employees and their perception of what working for Tesco is like. The position of migrant workers employed by the supermarket's suppliers is well covered, using evidence from the T&G and other sources, and justifiably highlighted as akin to 'modern-day slavery'. Exploitation of both land and factory workers in the South is comprehensively dealt with. The 256,000 UK employees of Tesco, however, nearly 60% of them women, scarcely get a mention. Are they really that quiescent? They shouldn't be if Simms is right: for example, proposals in China under their new Labour Contract Law are superior, in printed rights at least, to the present terms and conditions of Tesco's UK labour force.

This book is a damning critique of supermarkets in general and Tesco in particular. The case is well made and, although many of the arguments can be found elsewhere, it does come together as a comprehensive survey of the territory. It covers an awful lot of terrain from the ideas of the Slow Food Movement to the yawning and increasing disparities between the élite and the global commons, and, apart from perhaps its wistful approach to a bygone age of small shopkeeping, deserves praise for the cogency of its approach. Many of its ideas and themes deserve to be present in a 21st century socialist critique of the *new* capitalism. Whatever happened to the retail co-operative movement? And is George Monbiot right: 'No political challenge can be met by shopping'?

John Daniels

Bakers, Food & Allied Workers Union

Supporting workers in struggle Wherever they may be.

Joe Marino   General Secretary
Ronnie Draper   President
Jackie Barnwell   Vice President

Stanborough House, Great North Road, Stanborough,
Welwyn Garden City, Hertfordshire. AL8 7TA
Phone 01707 260150 & 01707 259450 | **www.bfawu.org**

Socialist Classics
www.spokesmanbooks.com

Studies in Socialism
Jean Jaurès

'This book consists of a number of essays, most of them centred on the method of transition from capitalism to socialism in the economically advanced countries ... The essays affirm strongly the case for democratic endeavour by socialists in seeking to change society.'
Jim Mortimer, Foreword to 2007 edition

£15.00 - paperback

Cromwell and Communism
Eduard Bernstein

Bernstein lives in the socialist folk-memory as the founder of "revisionism": admirers see him as a great innovator, while detractors still describe him as the "pope" of moderation. In reality, he had a radical mind, which is very well displayed in this still vibrant history of socialist and democratic thought in the English Revolution.

£15.00 - paperback

A History of British Socialism
Max Beer

Beer's *History* is a classic, not only because it is a brilliant pioneering study, but also because it is still urgently relevant to a new generation of socialists. Politics in modern Britain will make more sense to those who really study this book.

'It would be difficult to imagine a book more fair-minded than Mr Beer's, or showing more mastery of the voluminous material of his subject'
Bertrand Russell

£11.95 - large format, illustrated paperback